Butterflies 0–4

Count the butterflies in each frame. Trace the numbers.

0   0   0   0

1   1   1   1

2   2   2   2

3   3   3   3

4   4   4   4

Butterflies 0–4

How Many Dots?

Count the dots on each domino. Trace the numbers.

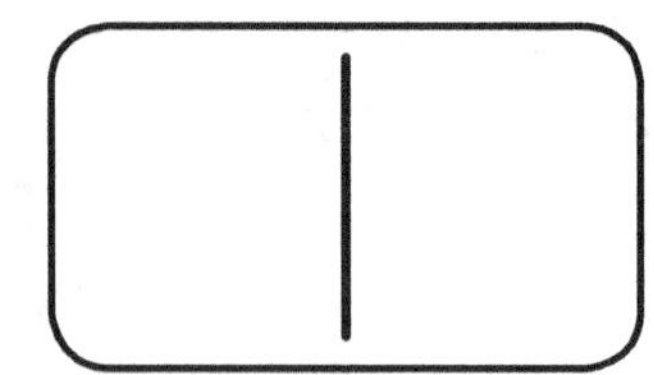 0 0 0 0 0

 1 1 1 1 1

 2 2 2 2 2

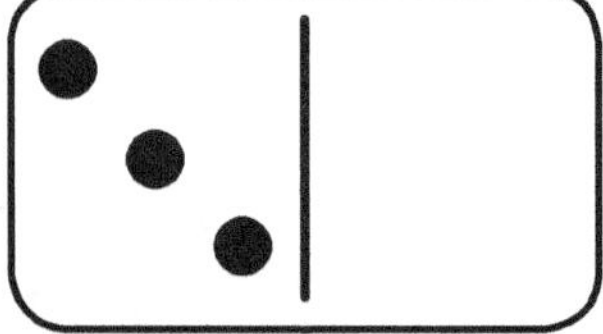 3 3 3 3 3

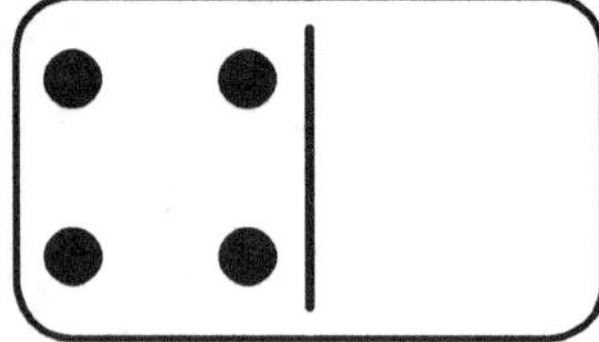 4 4 4 4 4

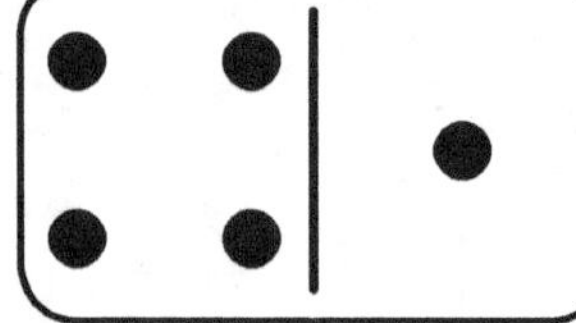 5 5 5 5 5

Find the Match Sheet 1

Draw a line to match the ten frame to the domino with the same number of dots.
Trace the numbers.

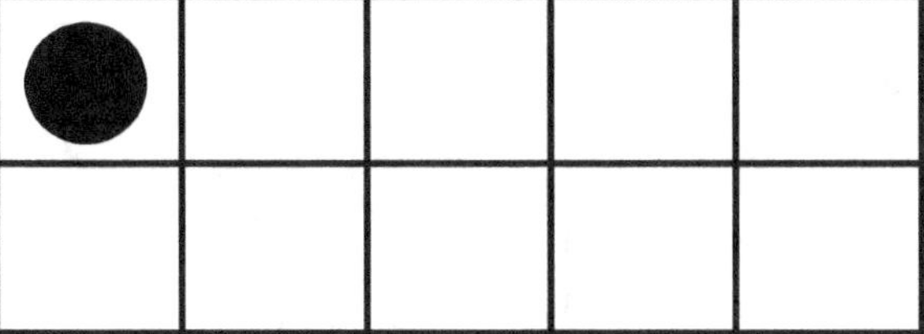 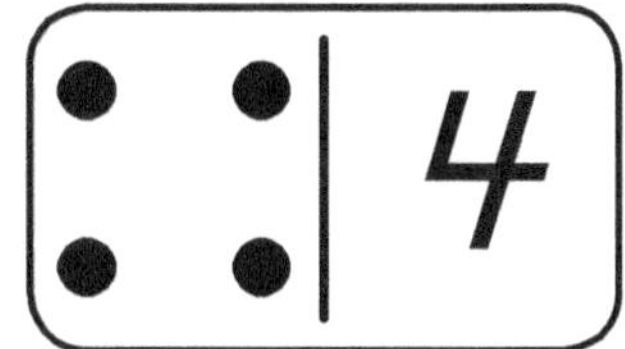 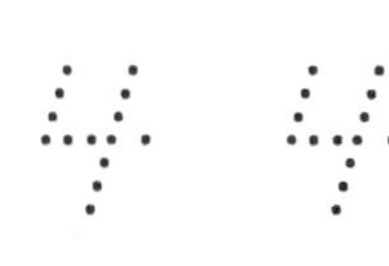

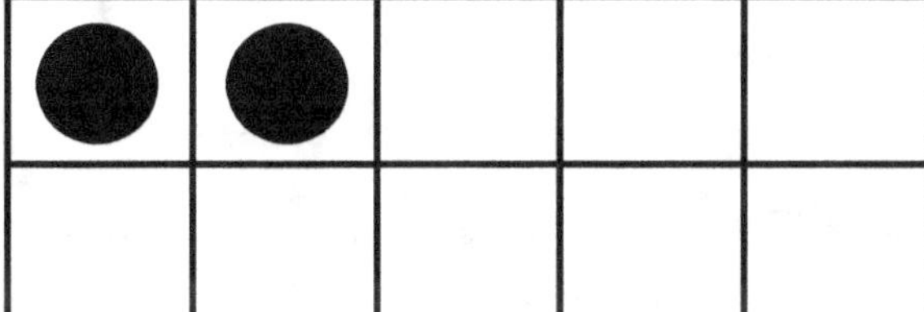 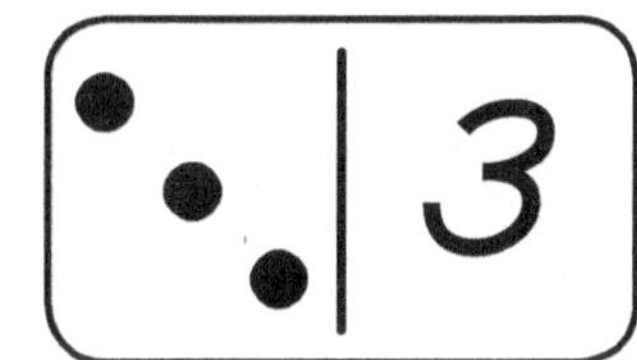 

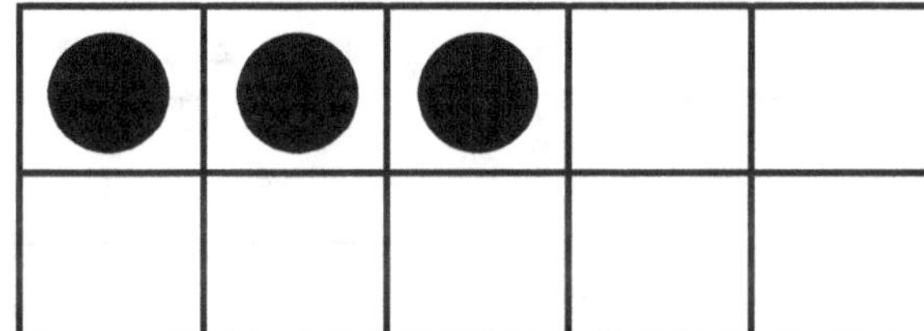 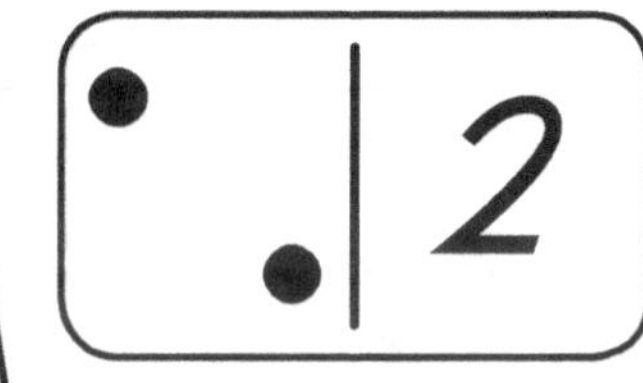 

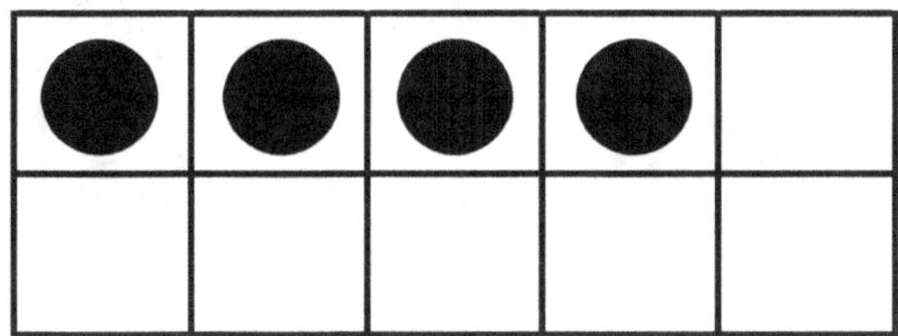 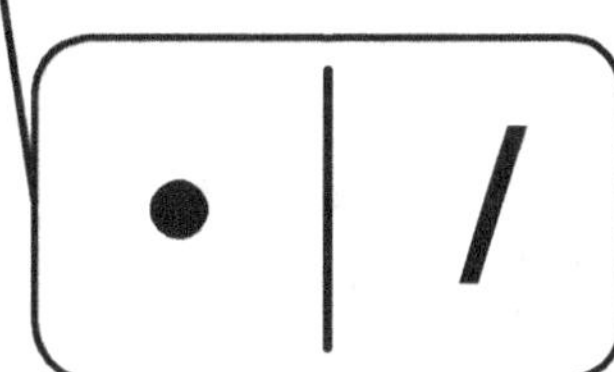 

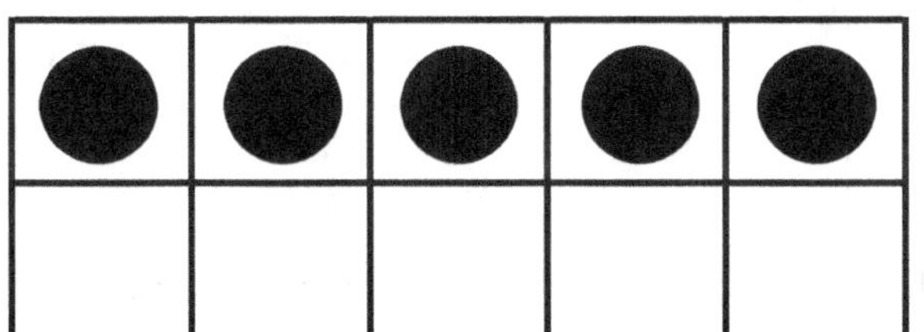  

Bugs in Boxes

Count the bugs in each box. Draw a line to the domino that has the same number. Trace the numbers.

1

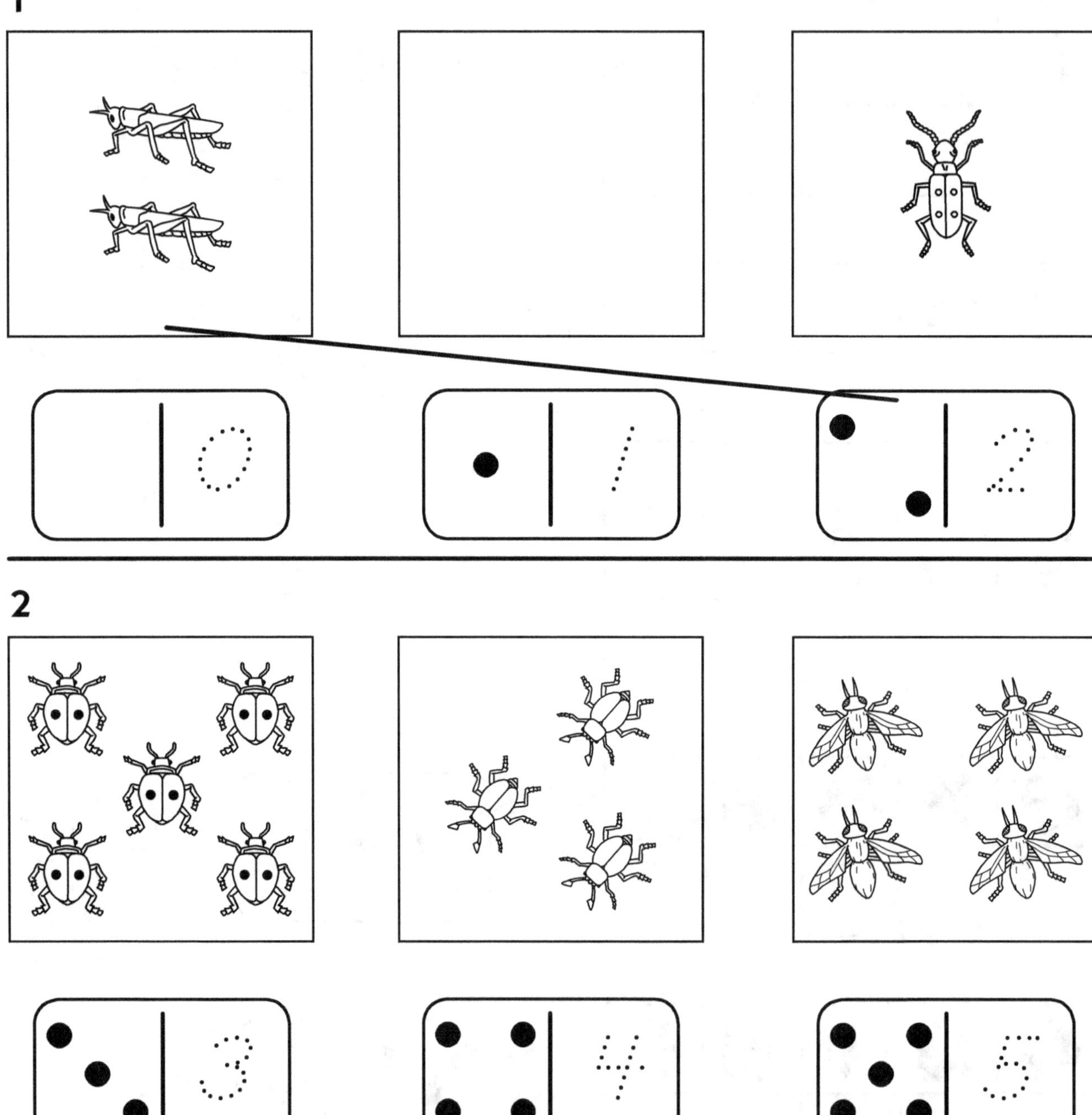

2

NAME ______________________ DATE ____________

Sets & Numbers Match

1 Draw a line to match each set to the number that tells how many. Trace the number three times..

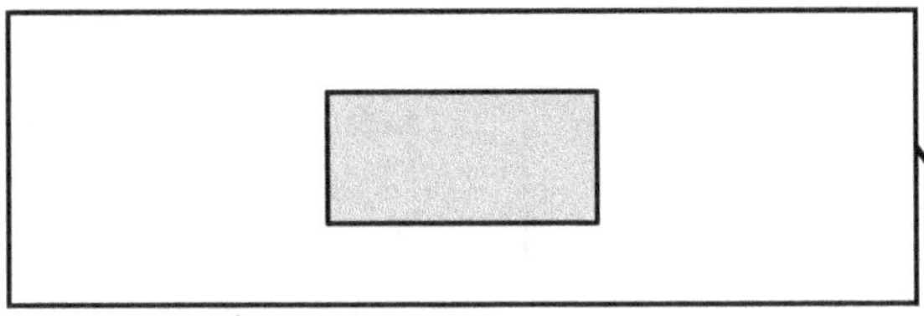

3 circles

3 3 3

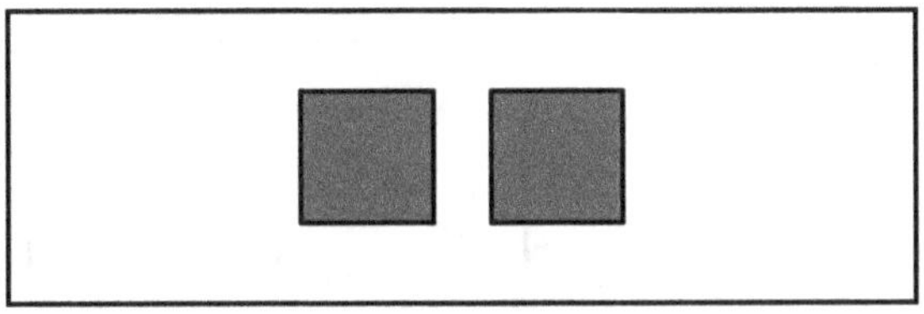

1 rectangle

1 1 1

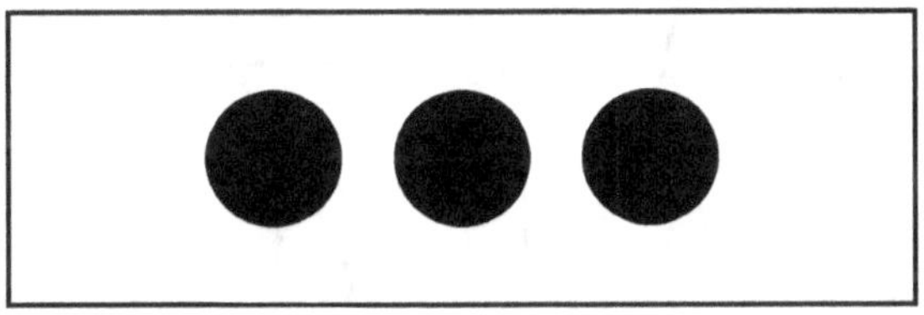

4 stars

4 4 4

2 squares

2 2 2

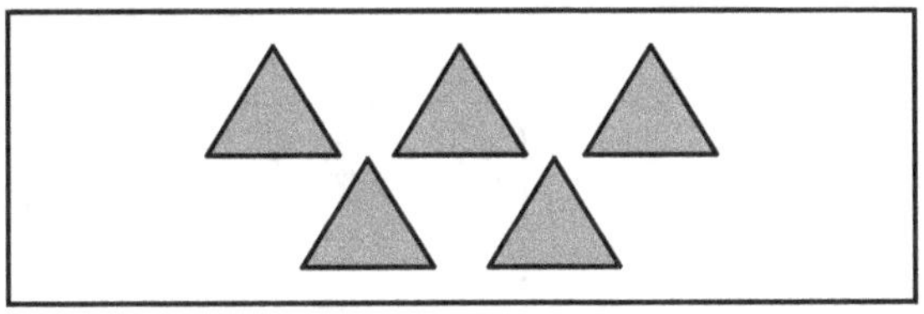

5 triangles

5 5 5

2 Trace the numbers below.

0 1 2 3 4 5

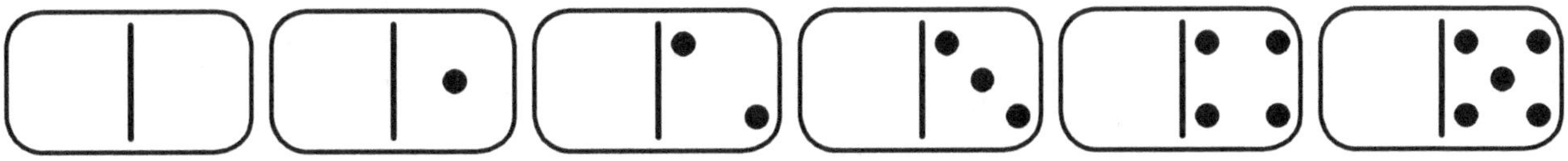

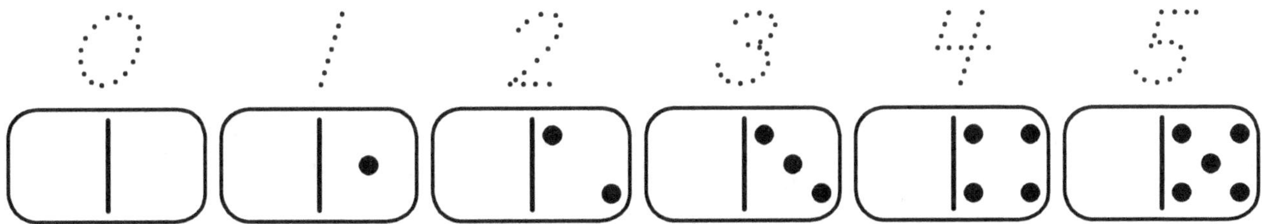

Counting Cubes

Color the cubes as indicated. Draw a line to the domino that has the same number. Trace the numbers.

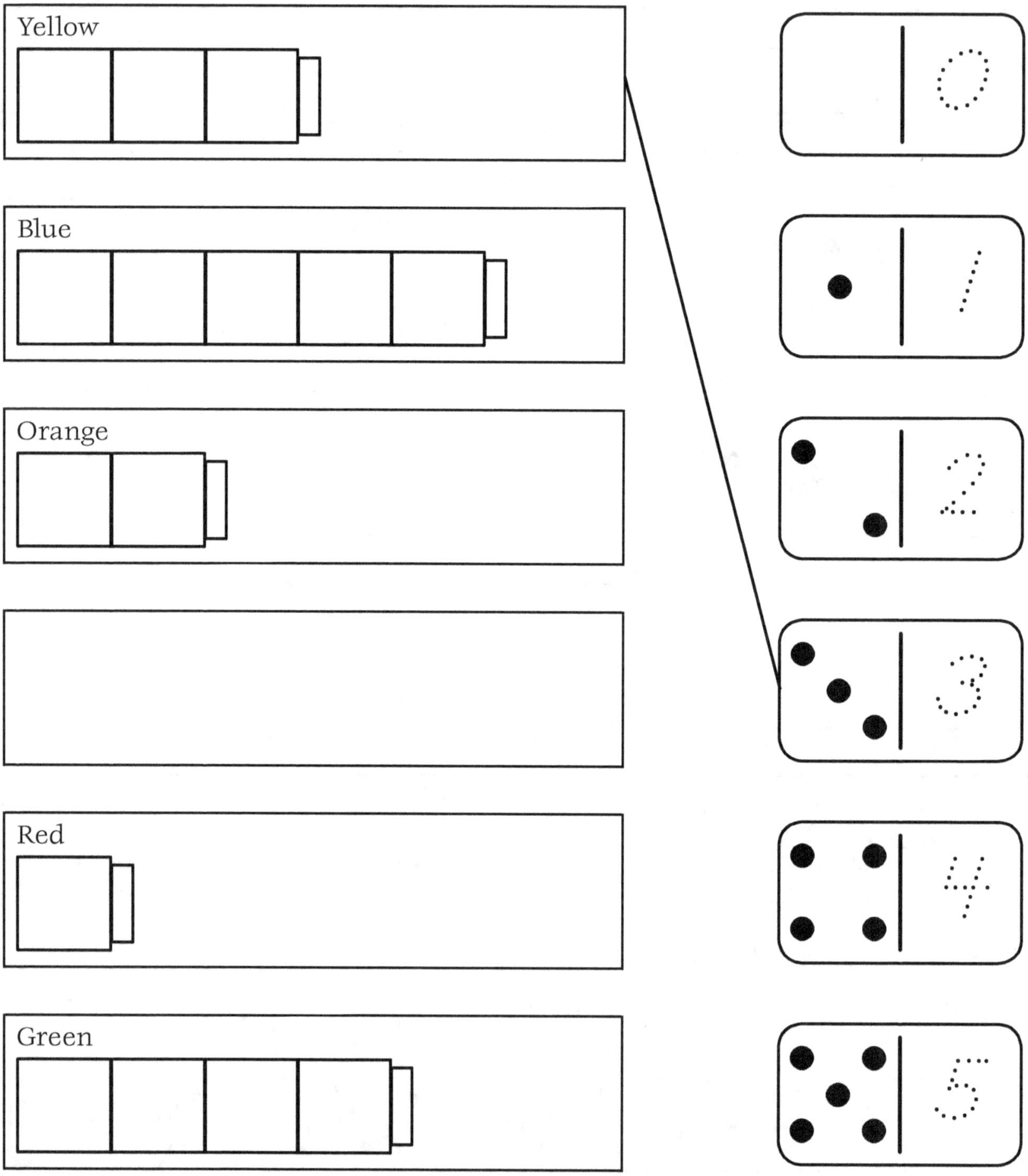

Yellow

Blue

Orange

Red

Green

Shapes & Numbers

1 Color the number of shapes as indicated below.

Color 5 squares:

Color 4 rectangles:

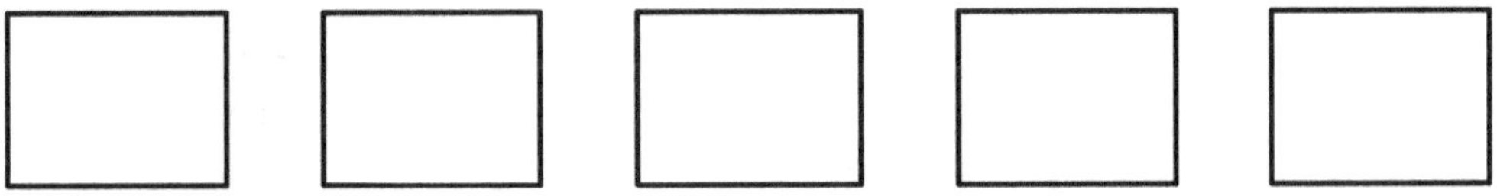

Color 2 triangles:

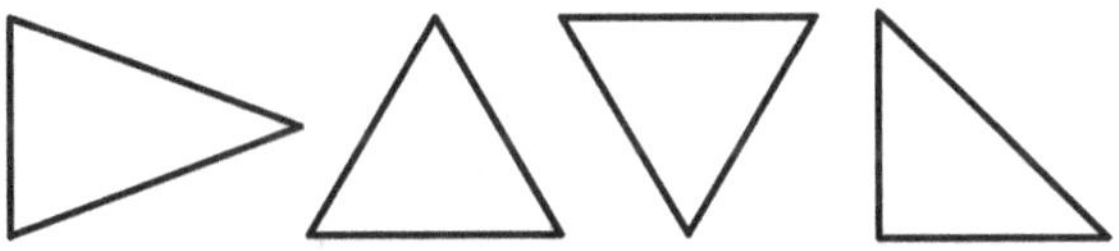

Color 3 circles:

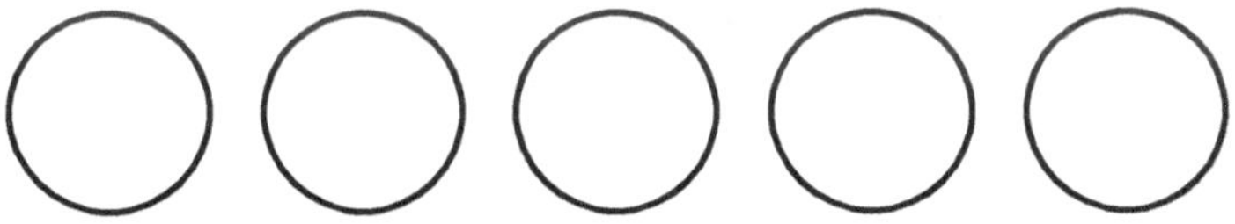

2 Trace the numbers.

Triangles, Squares & Rectangles How Many Sides?

1 Trace the numbers.

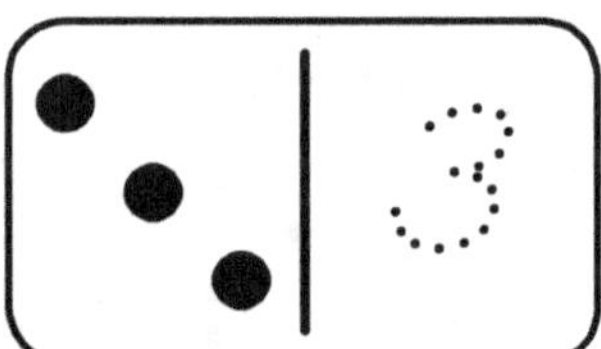 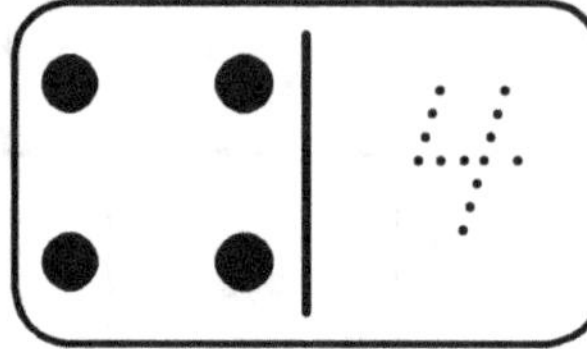 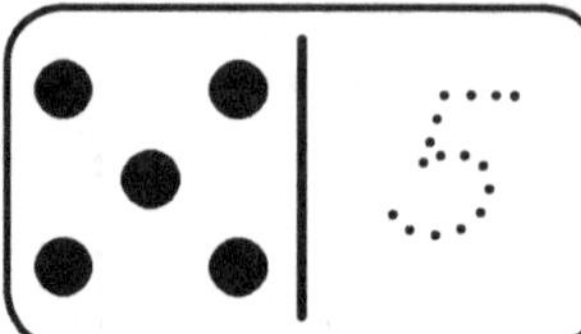 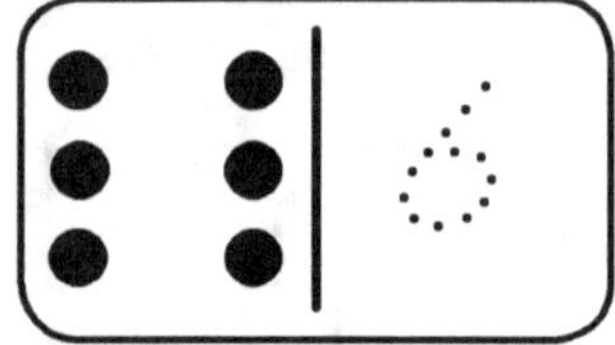

2 Count and record the number of sides on each shape. You can add an arrow on each side if it helps.

Triangle How many sides?	Triangle How many sides?
Rectangle How many sides?	Square How many sides?
Triangle How many sides?	Rectangle How many sides?
Square How many sides?	**CHALLENGE** Hexagon How many sides?

Triangles, Squares & Rectangles How Many Corners?

1 Trace the numbers.

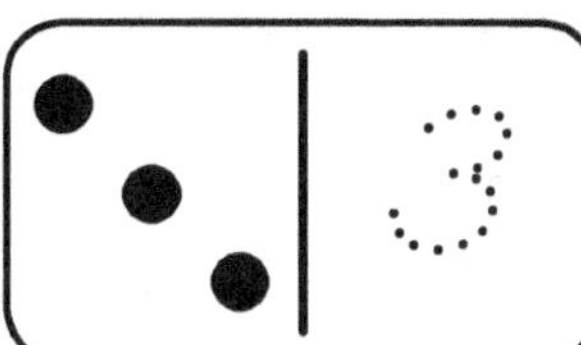 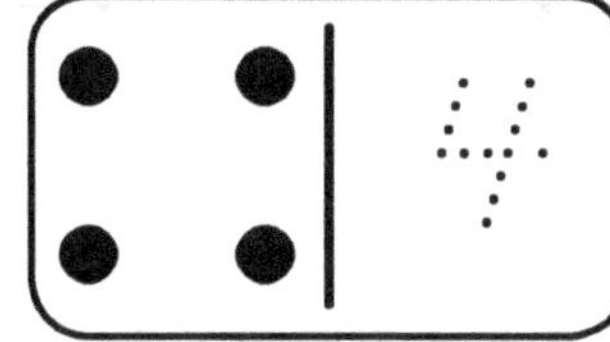 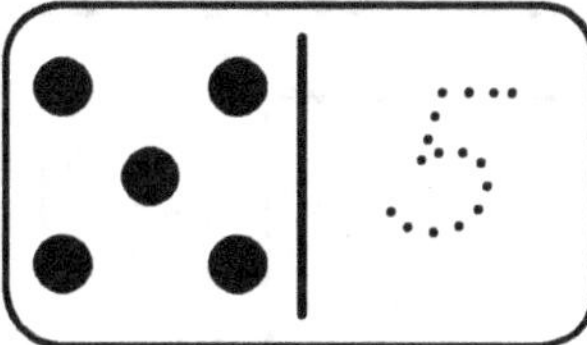 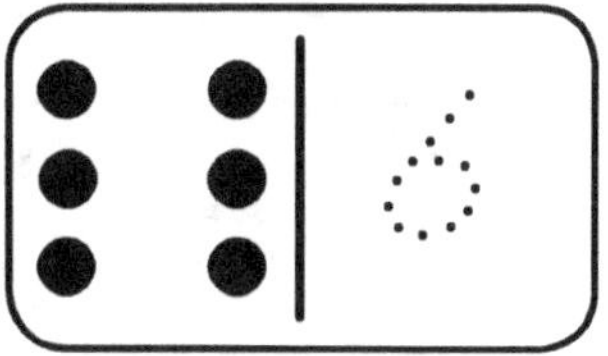

2 Count and record the number of corners on each shape. You can add an arrow at each corner if it helps.

Triangle — How many corners?	Triangle — How many corners?
Rectangle — How many corners?	Square — How many corners?
Triangle — How many corners?	Rectangle — How many corners?
Square — How many corners?	**CHALLENGE** Hexagon — How many corners?

Ladybugs 5–9

Count the ladybugs in each frame. Trace the numbers.

More Dots

Count the dots on each domino. Trace the numbers.

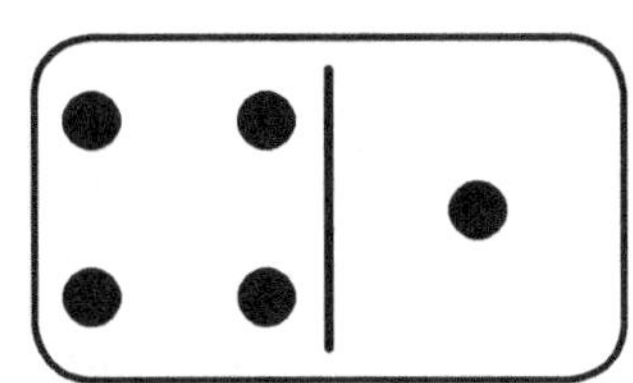 5  5 5 5 5

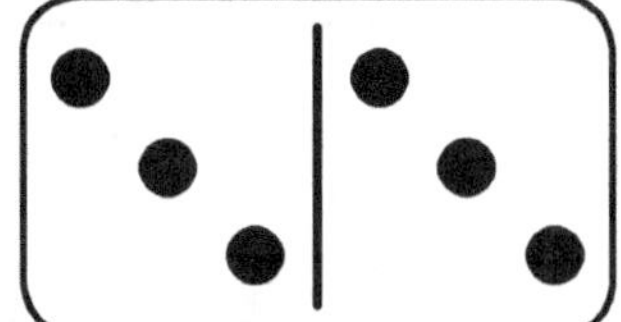 6  6 6 6 6

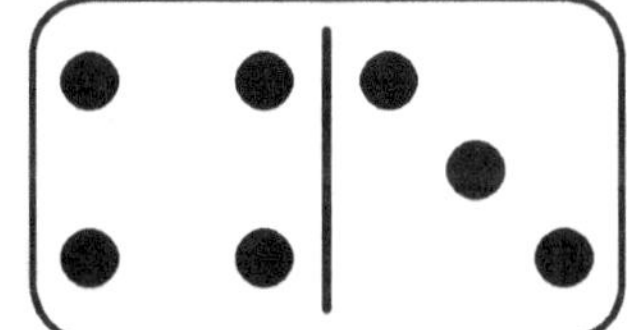 7 7 7 7 7

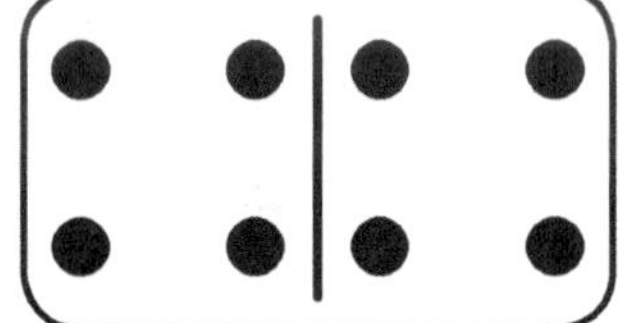 8  8 8 8 8

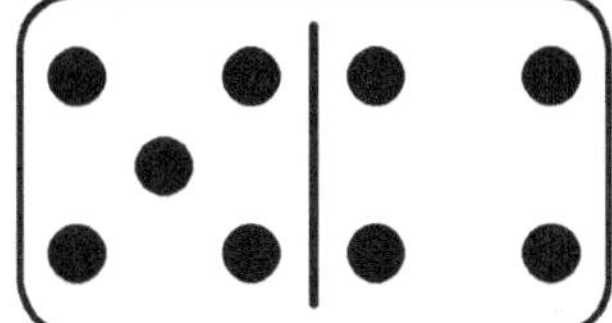 9 9 9 9 9

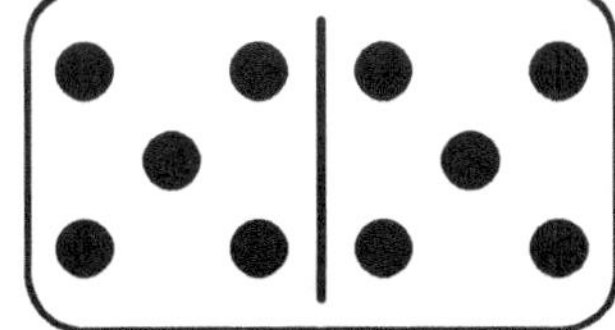 10 10 10 10 10

Shape Patterns

Draw the 3 shapes you think should come next in each pattern below.

1

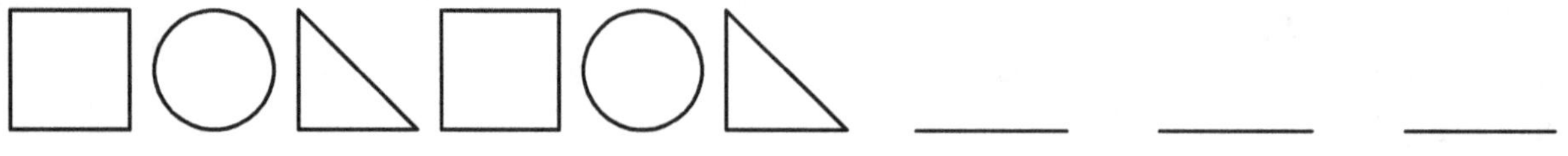

2

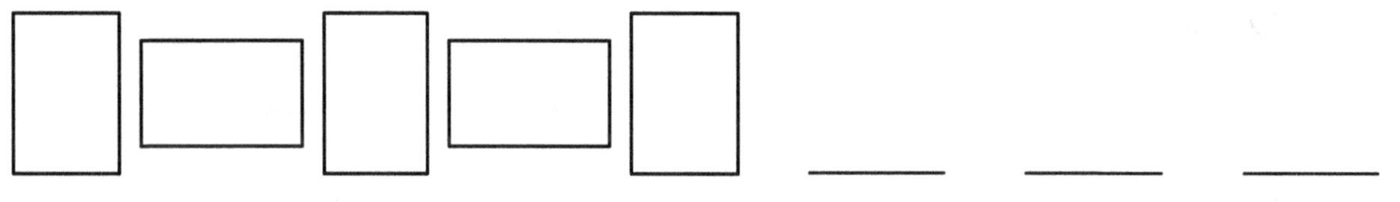

3

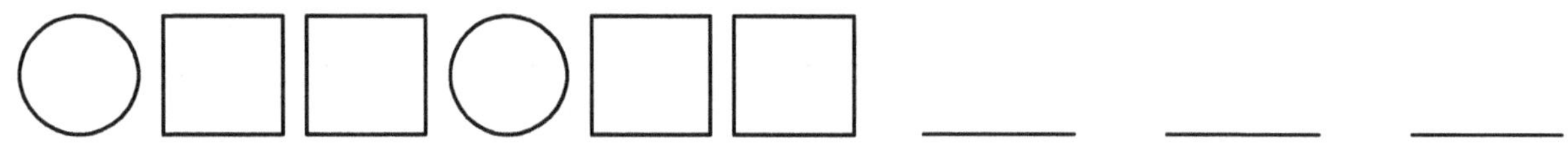

4

5

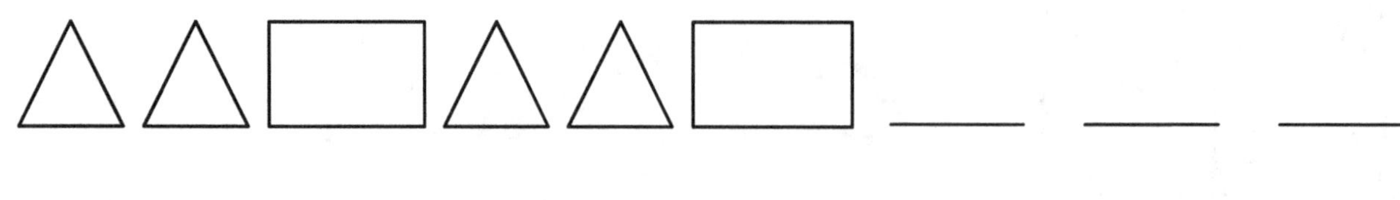

Find the Match Sheet 2

Draw a line to match the ten frame to the domino with the same number of dots.
Trace the numbers.

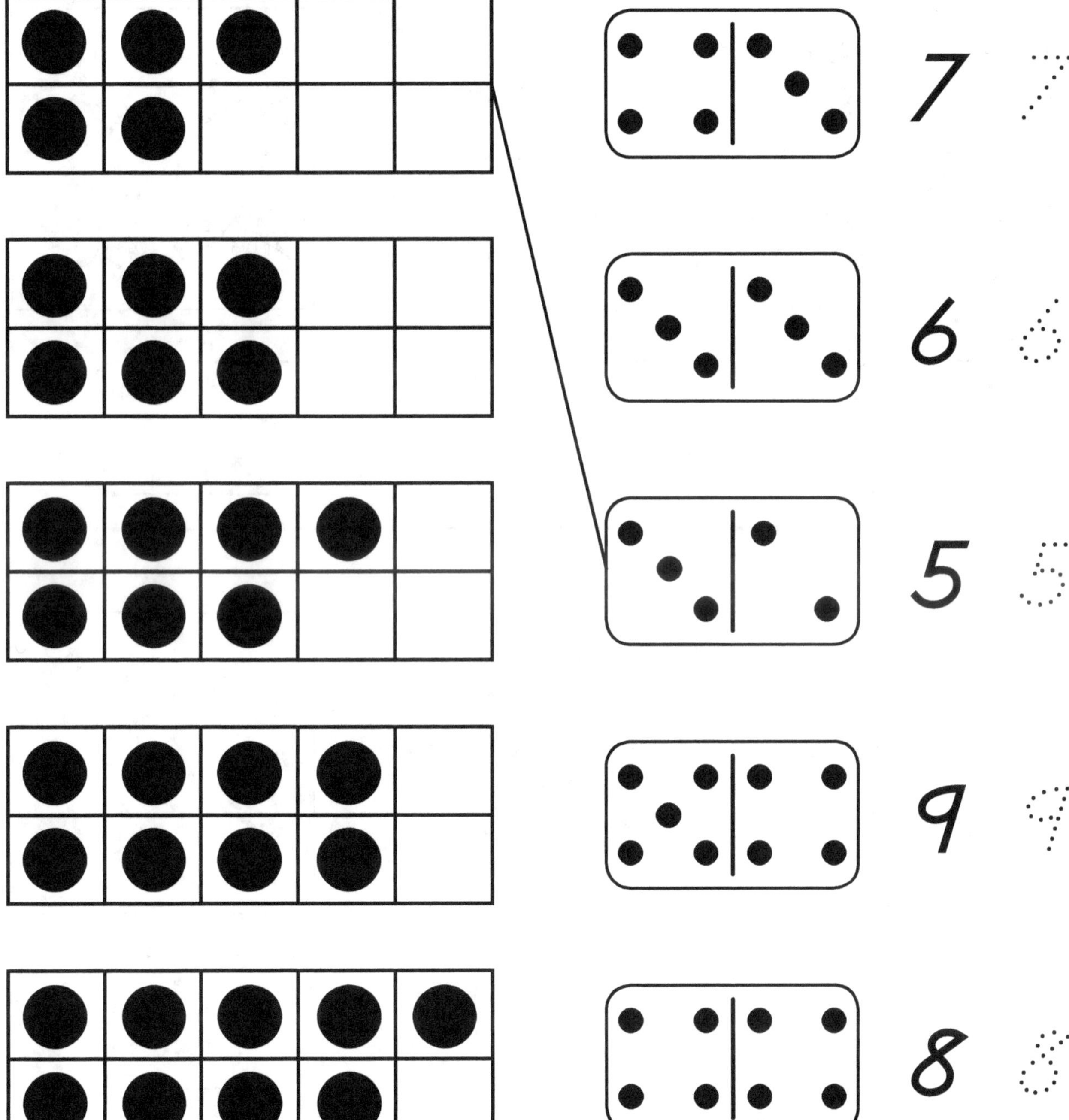

More Bugs in Boxes

Count the bugs in each box. Draw a line to the domino that has the same number.
Trace the numbers.

1

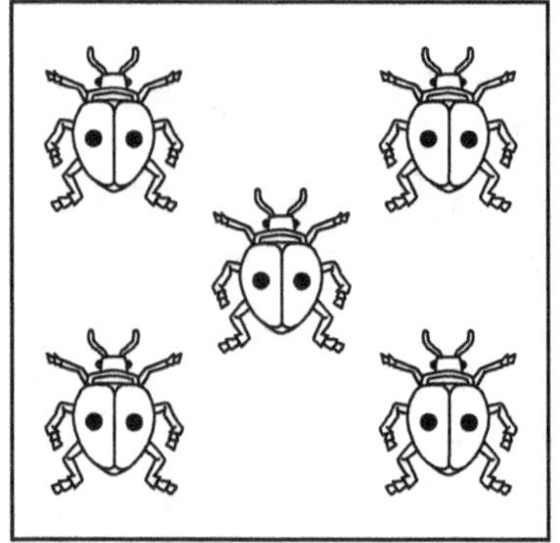 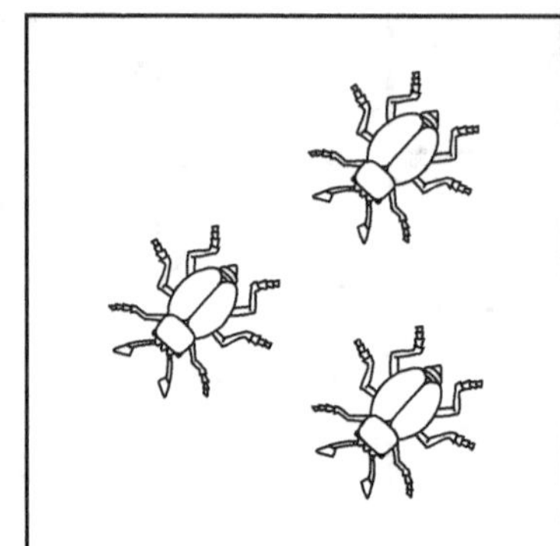 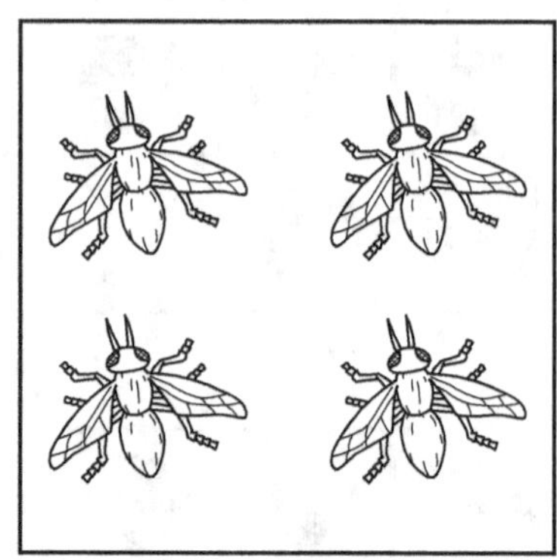

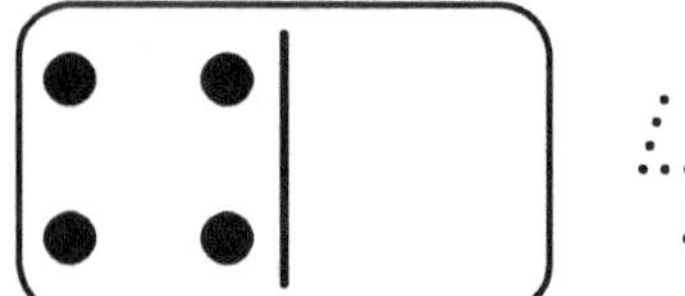 4   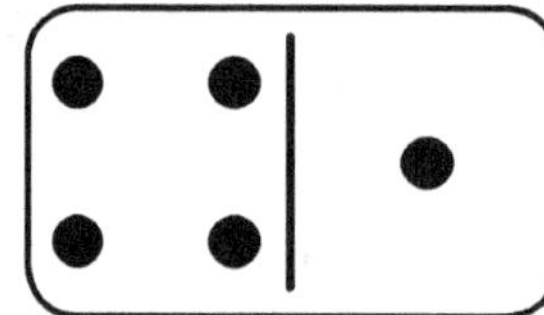  5   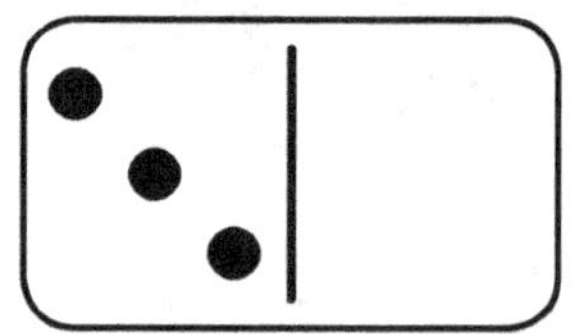 3

2

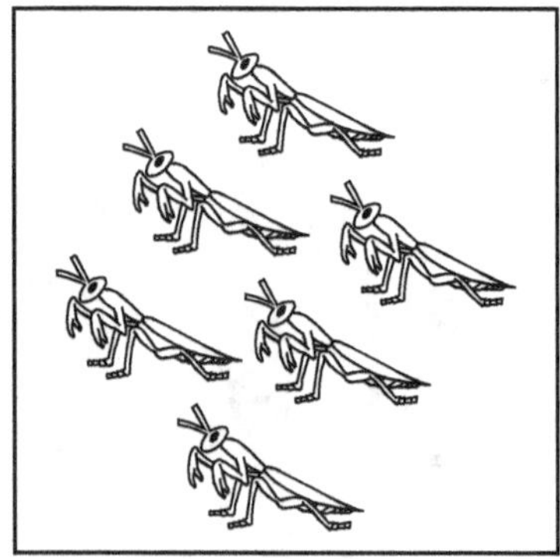  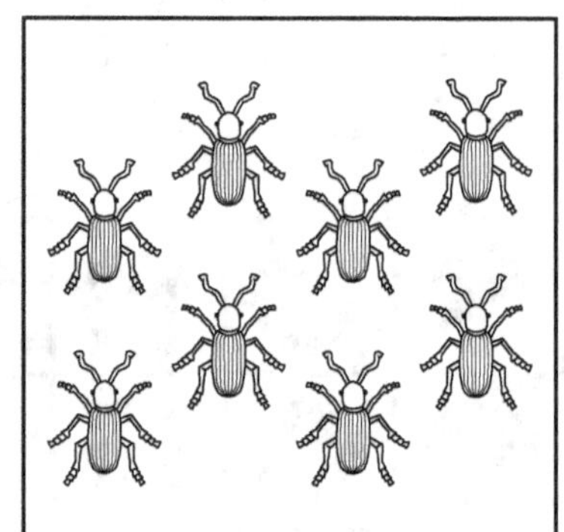

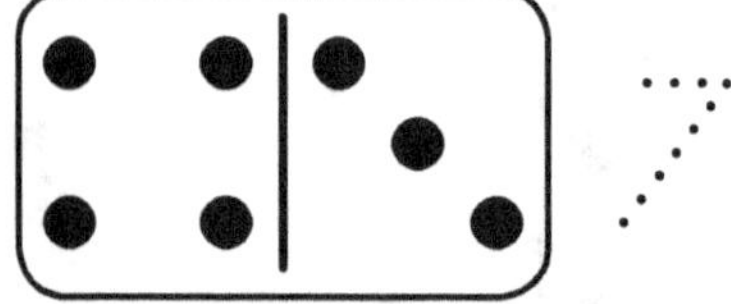 7   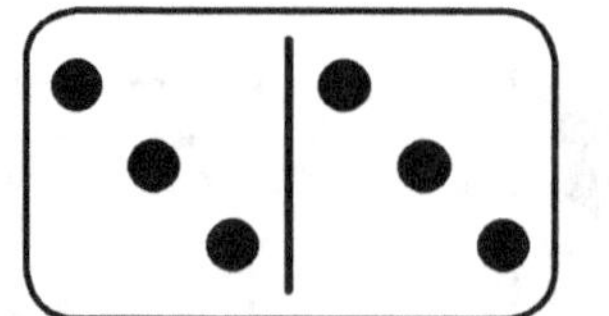 6   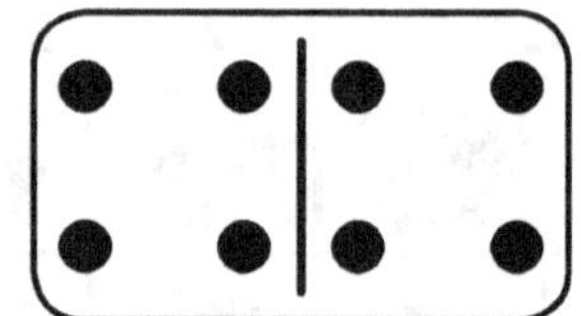  8

Fill the Boxes

1 Trace the numbers.

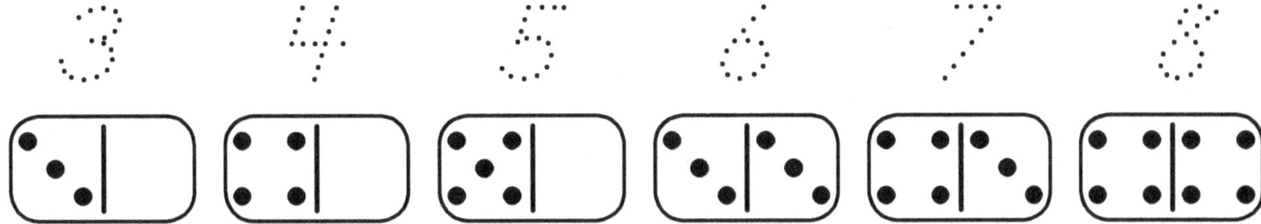

2 Draw the items below.

Draw 3 bugs. 	
Draw 4 dots.	
Draw 5 lines.	
Draw 6 eggs. 	
Draw 7 hearts. 	

Dot-to-Dot

1 Trace the numbers. Draw a line from each number to the matching domino.

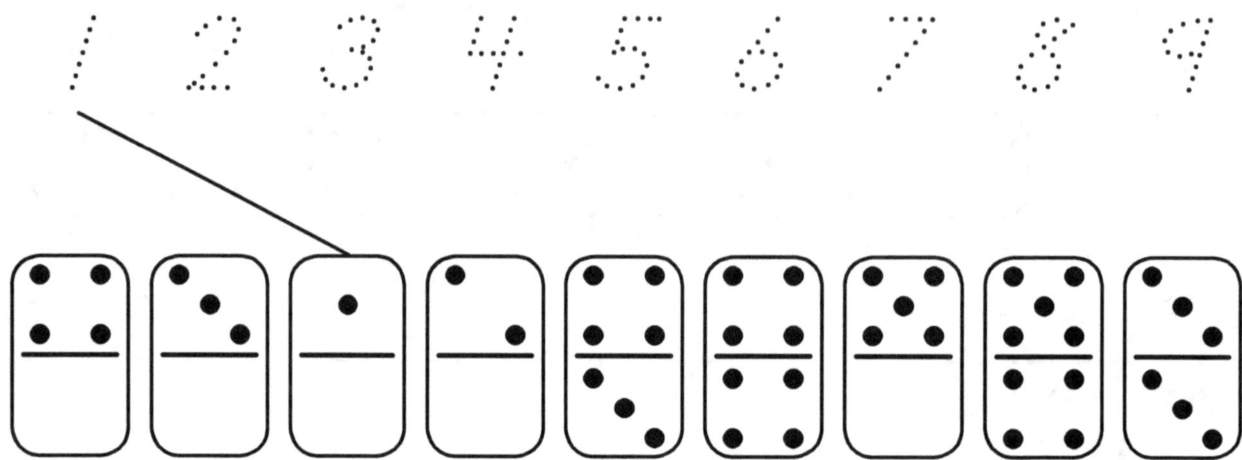

2 Trace the numbers. Connect the dots in order to make a picture.

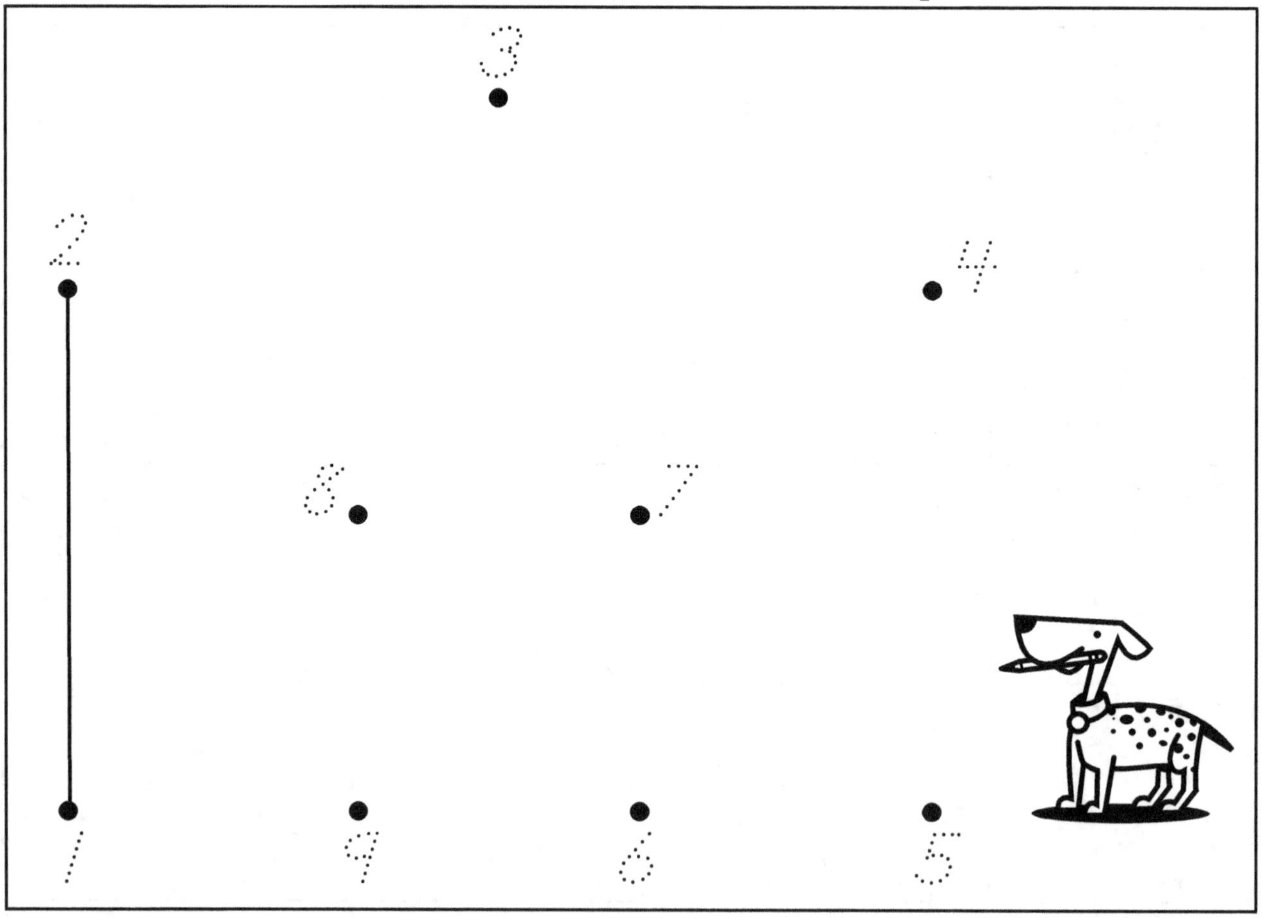

Patterns What Comes Next?

1 Draw or color what you think comes next in the pattern.

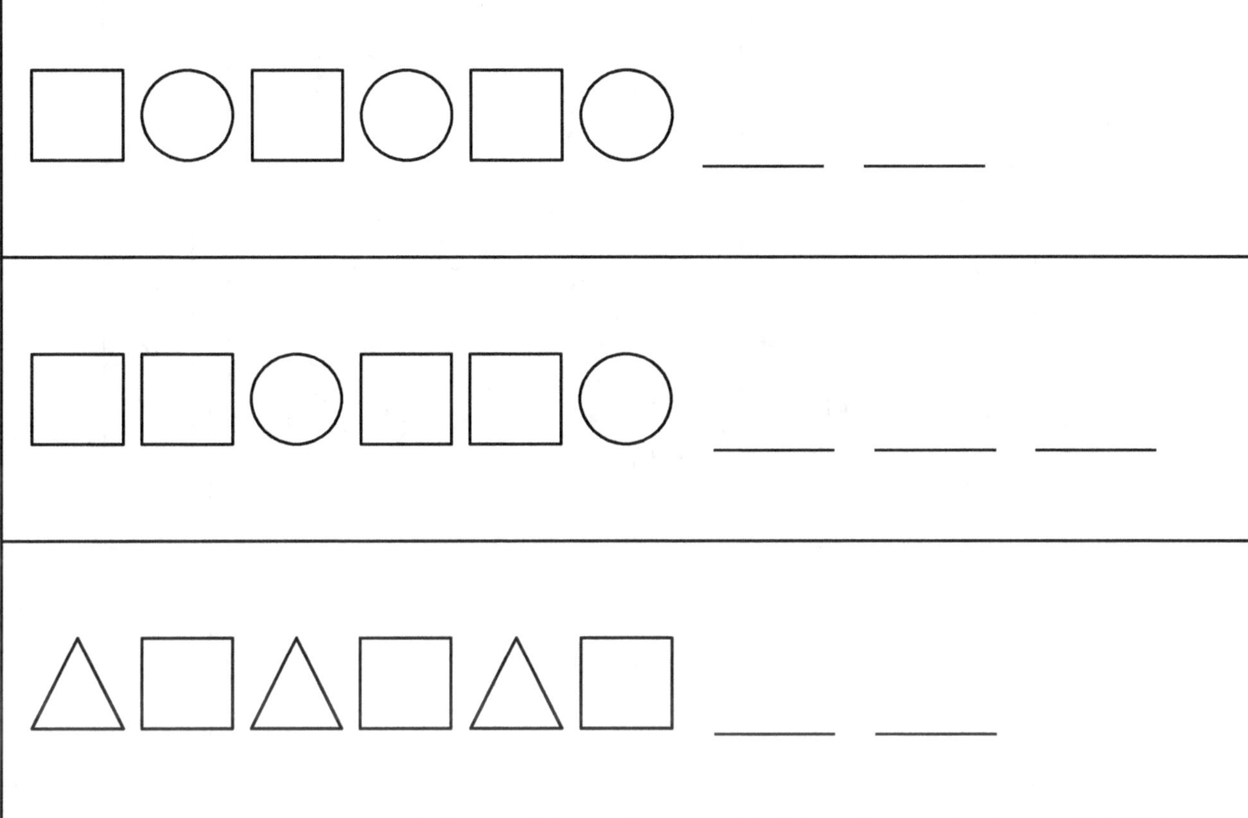

2 Fill in the numbers that are missing.

1 ____ 3 4 5 ____ 7 8 ____ 10

NAME ______________________ DATE ______________

How Many? Sheet 1

Use the numbers and the dominoes to help solve the problems below.

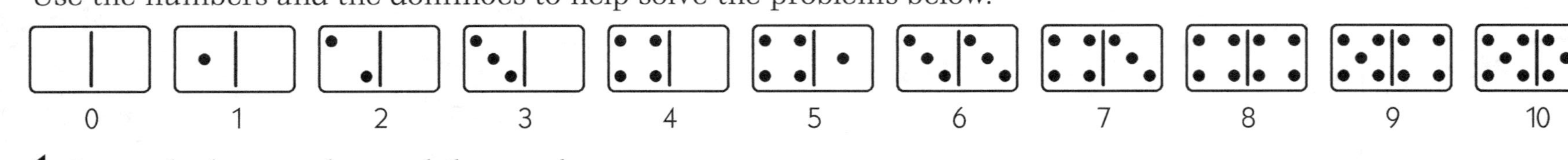

0 1 2 3 4 5 6 7 8 9 10

1 Count the bugs and record the number.

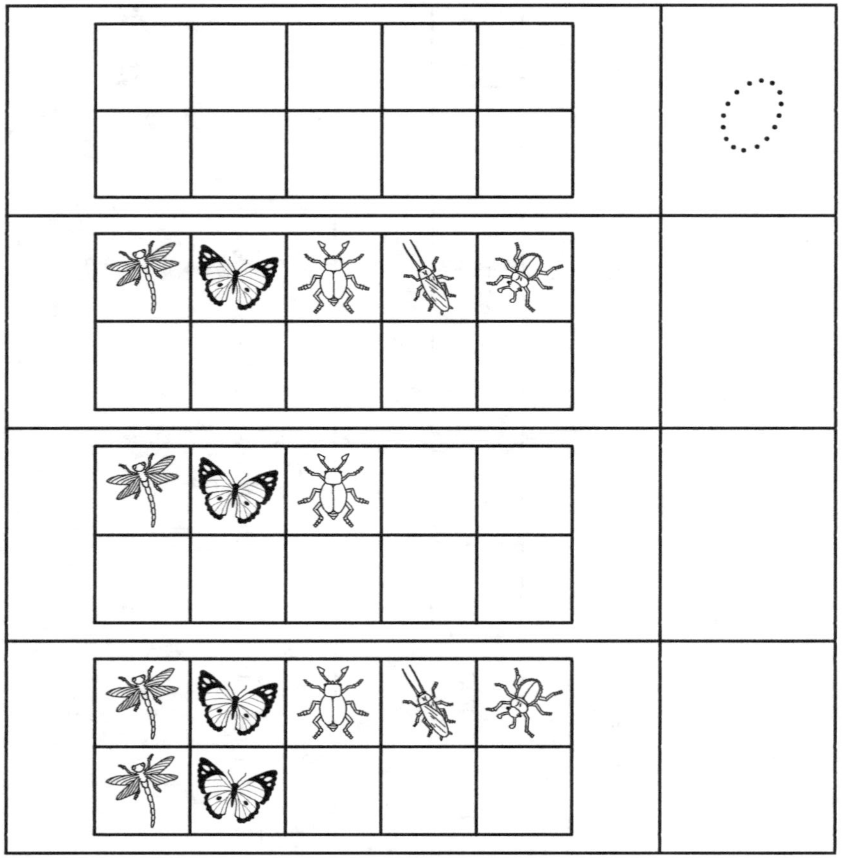

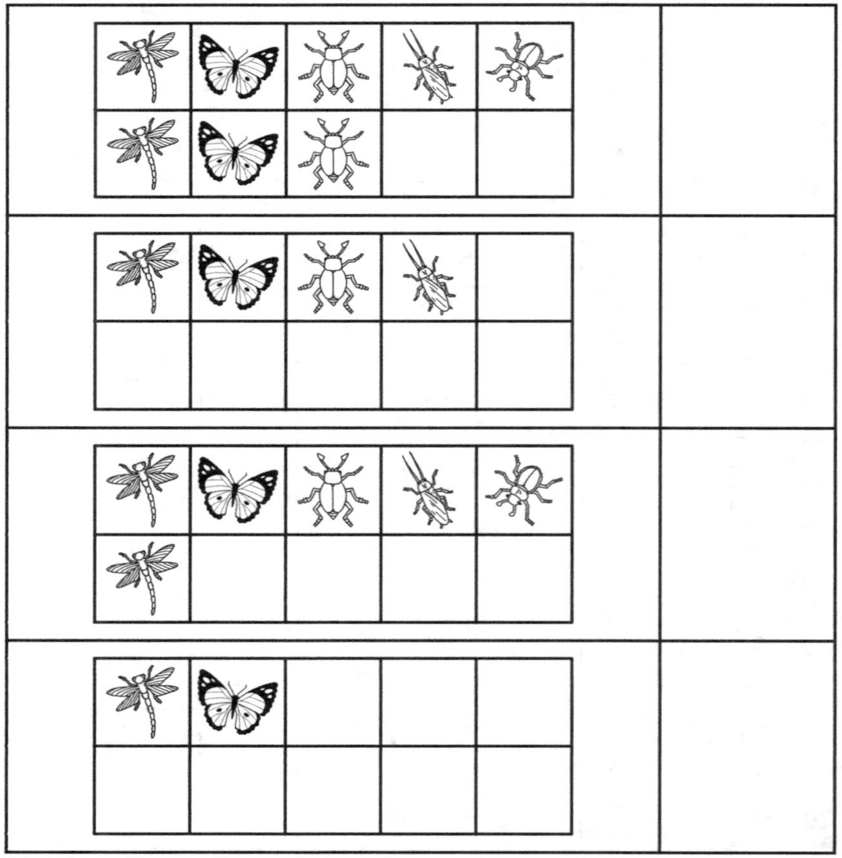

NAME ______________________ DATE ______________

Tallying How Many Sticks?

Use the numbers and dominoes to help solve the problems below.

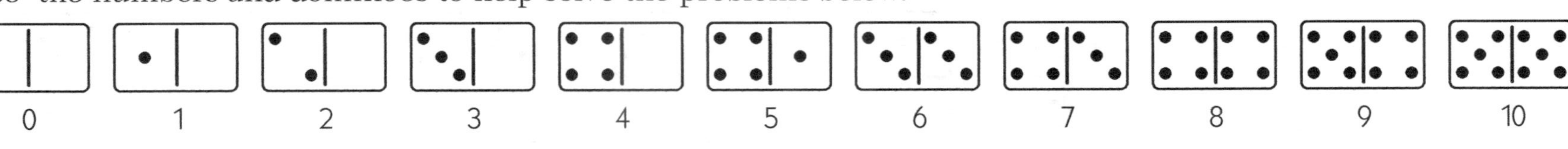

0
1
2
3
4
5
6
7
8
9
10

1 Count the number of sticks and record the number.

3

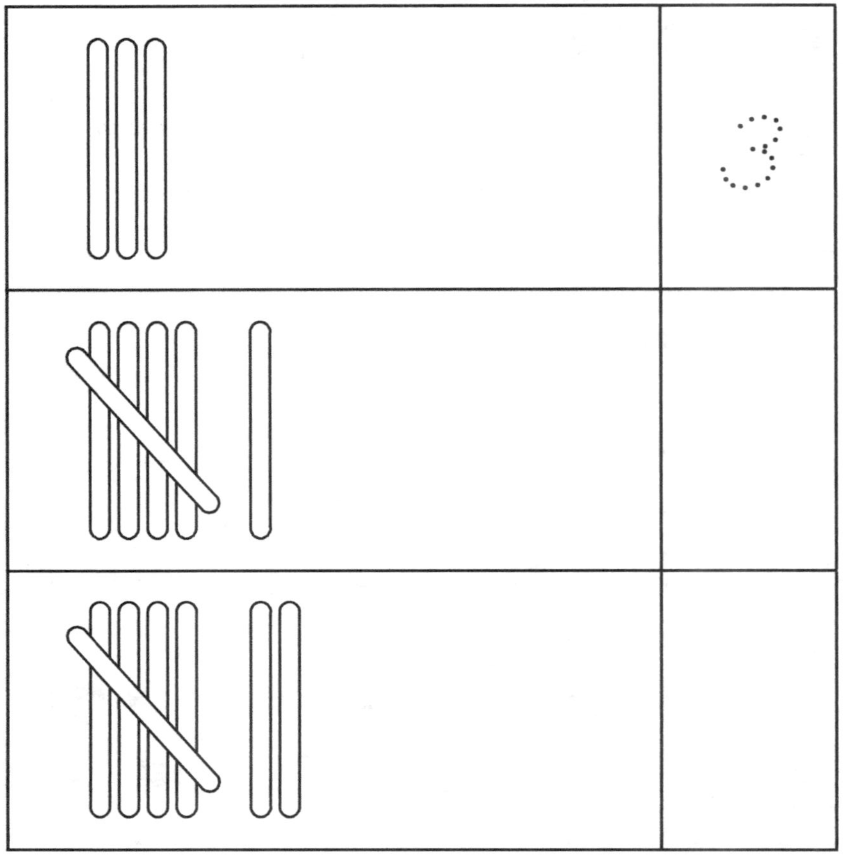

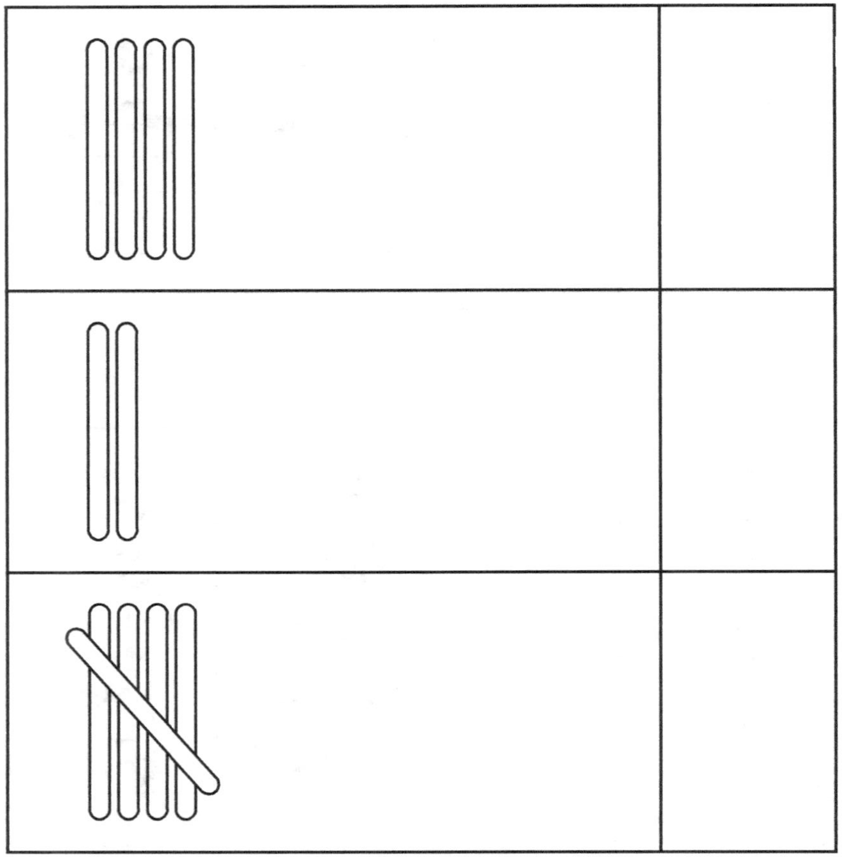

How Many? Sheet 2

Use the numbers to help solve the problems below.

0   1   2   3   4   5   6   7   8   9   10

Count the number of dots and record the number.

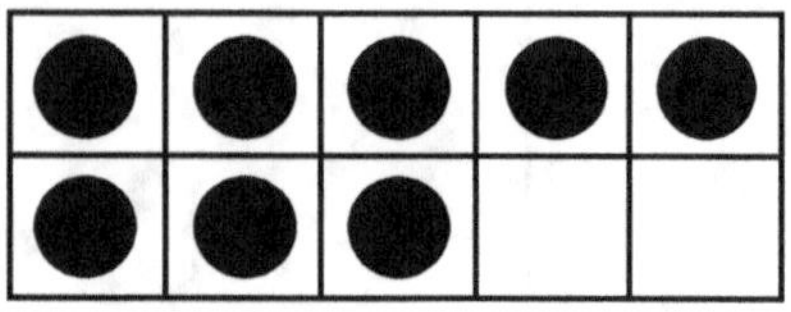

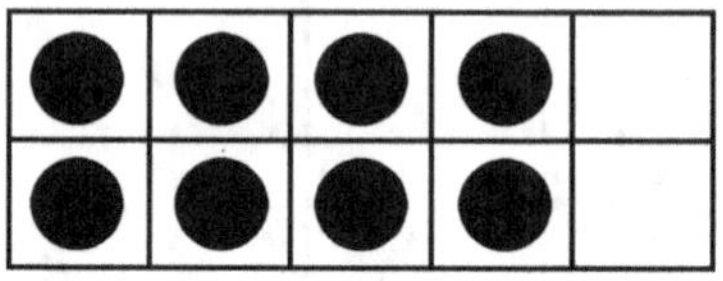

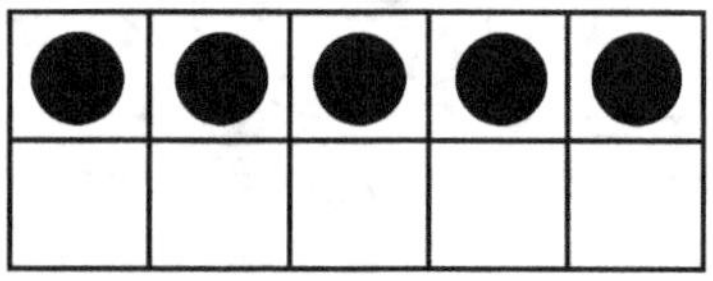

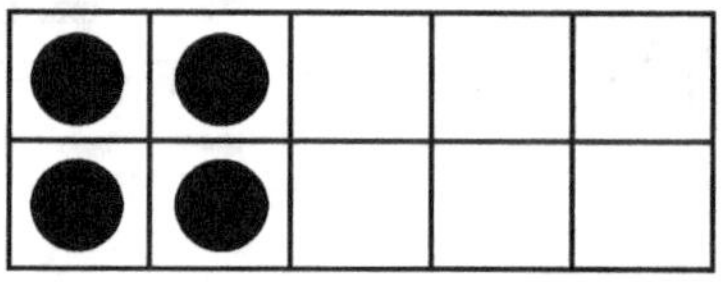

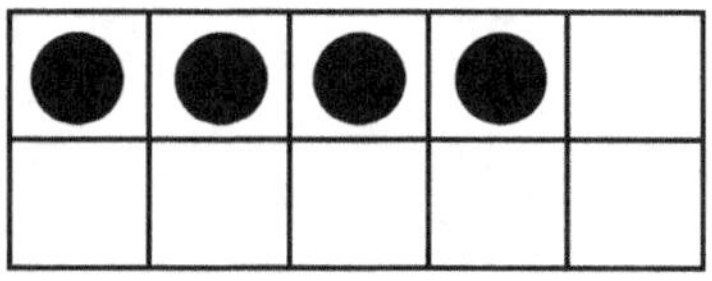

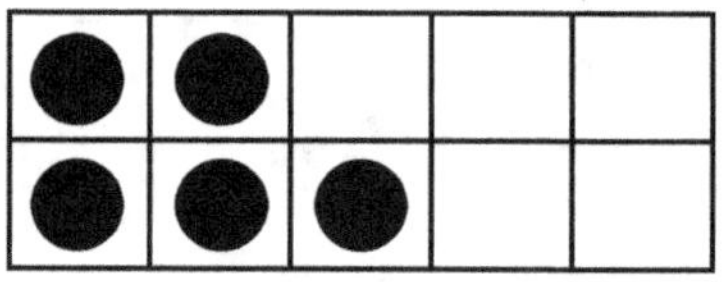

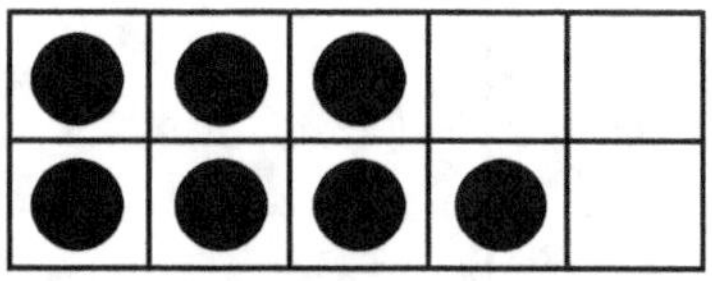

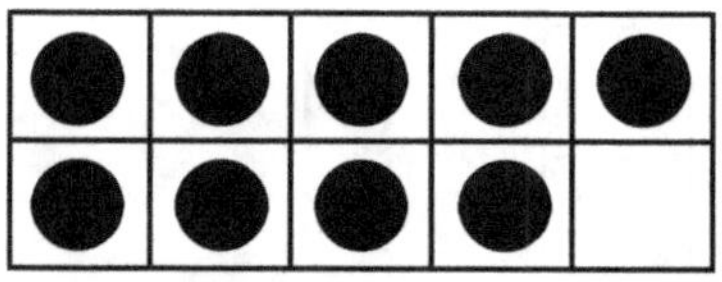

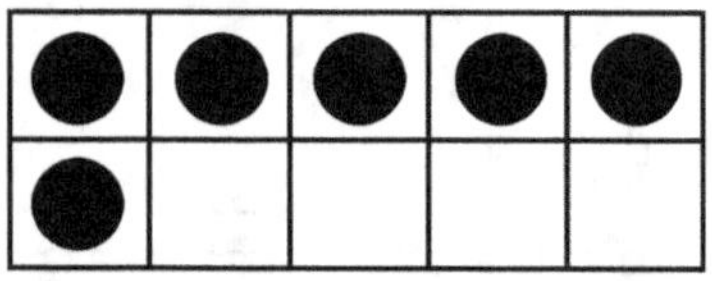

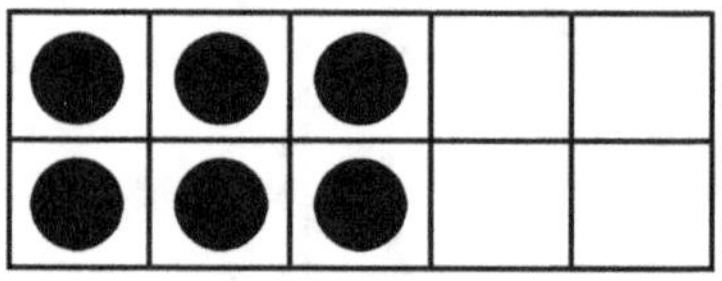

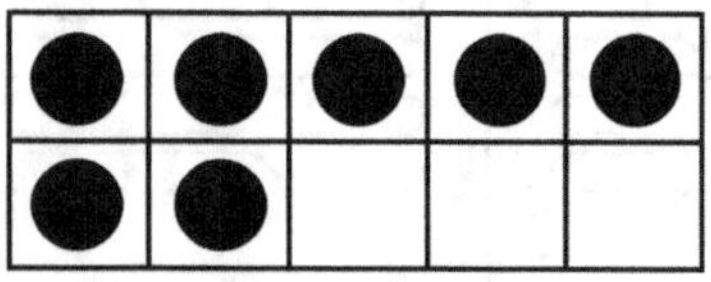

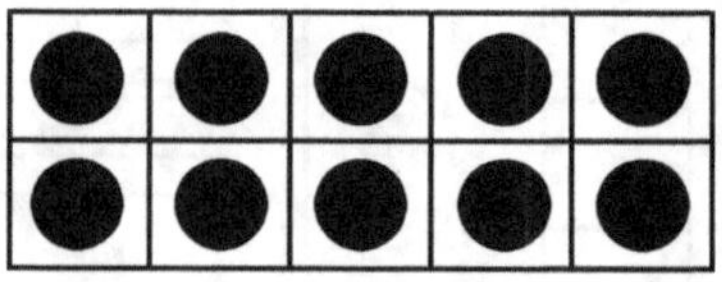

Can You Find the Match?

Draw a line from the ten frame to the tally sticks that match.

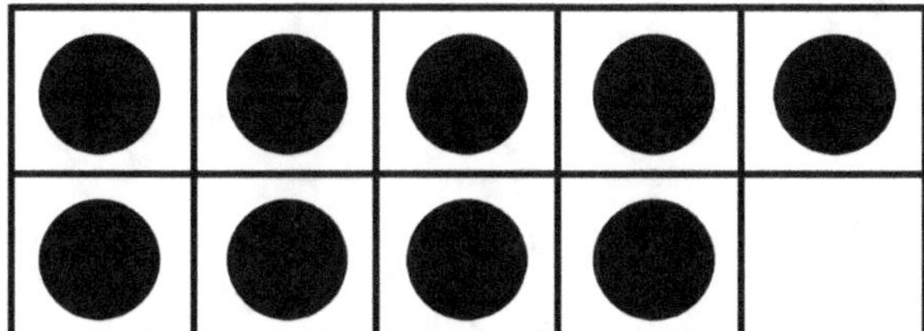

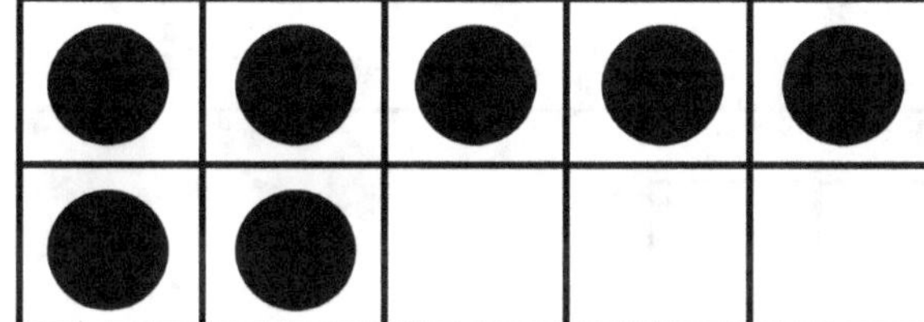

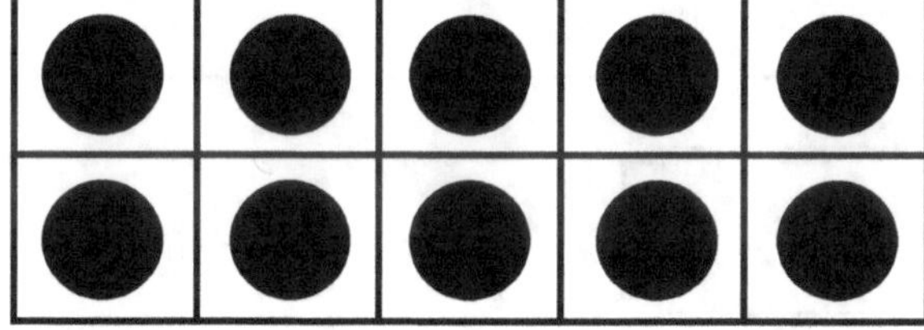

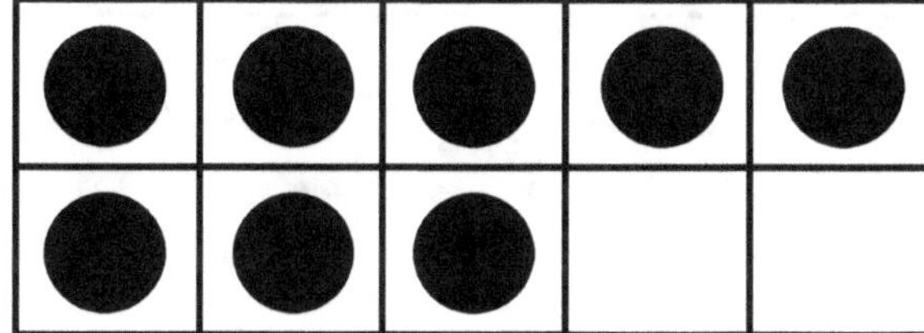

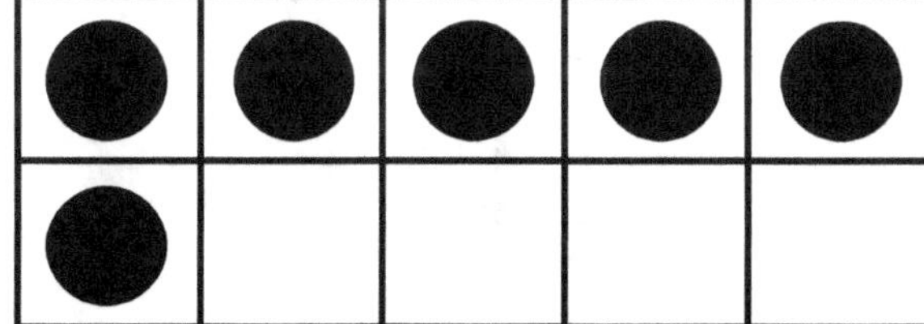

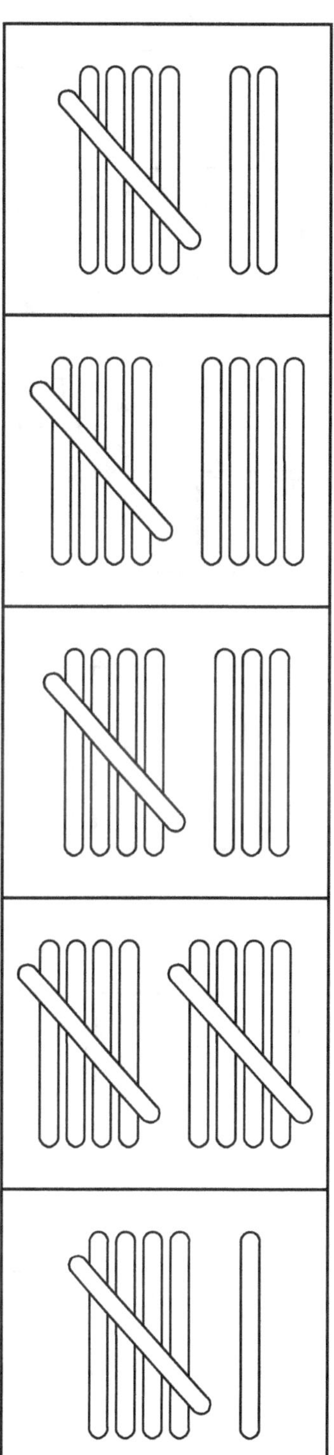

Adding One More

Use the numbers to help solve the problems below.

0   1   2   3   4   5   6   7   8   9   10

Solve the addition problems. Use the pictures to help.

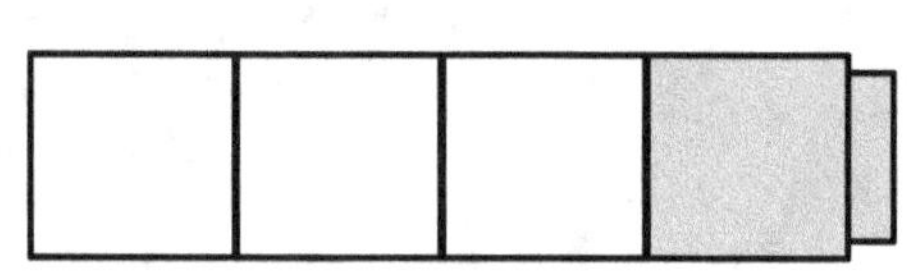

3 + 1 = _______

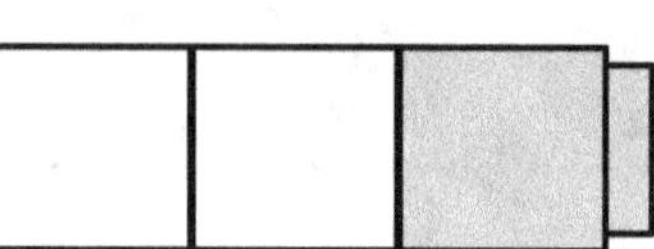

2 + 1 = _______

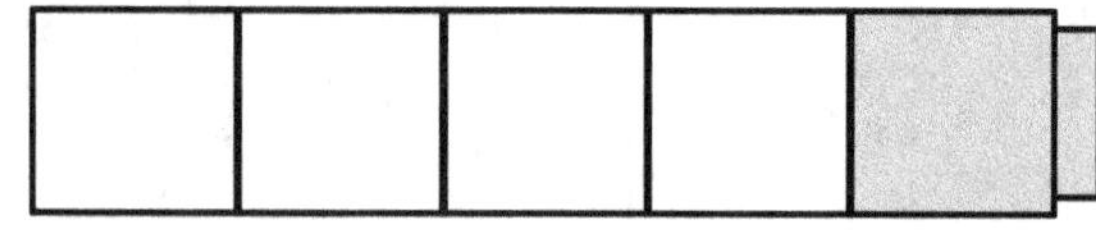

4 + 1 = _______

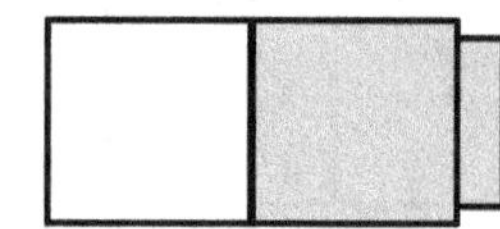

1 + 1 = _______

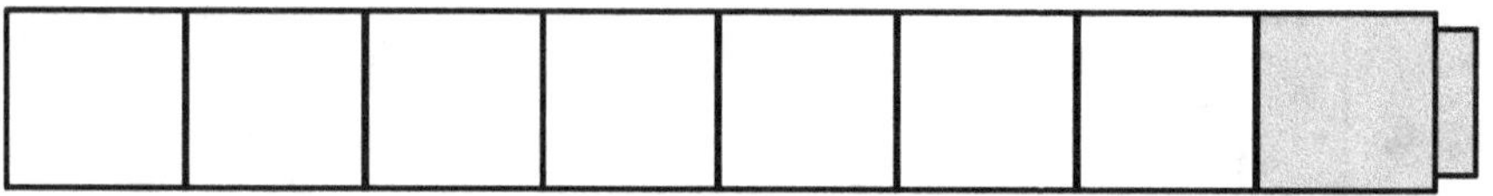

7 + 1 = _______

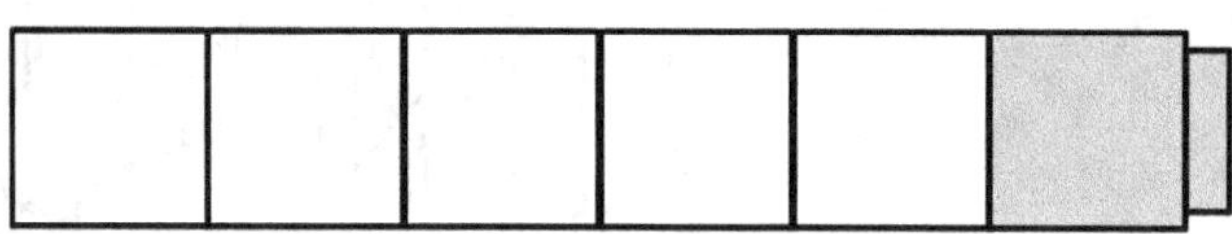

5 + 1 = _______

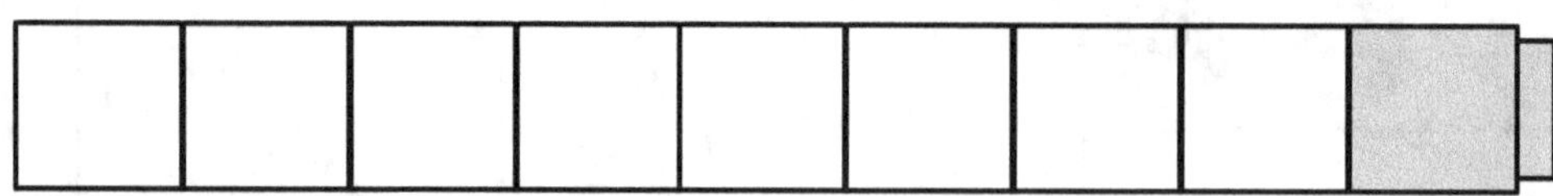

8 + 1 = _______

Butterfly Countdown Subtract One

Solve the subtraction problems. Use the pictures to help.

10 – 1 = _______

8 – 1 = _______

4 – 1 = _______

6 – 1 = _______

7 – 1 = _______

2 – 1 = _______

Add a Circle

Trace the numbers and complete the addition problems below. Use the pictures to help.

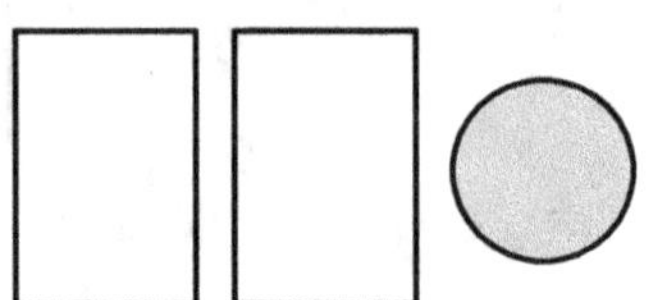 

$2 + 1 = \underline{3}$

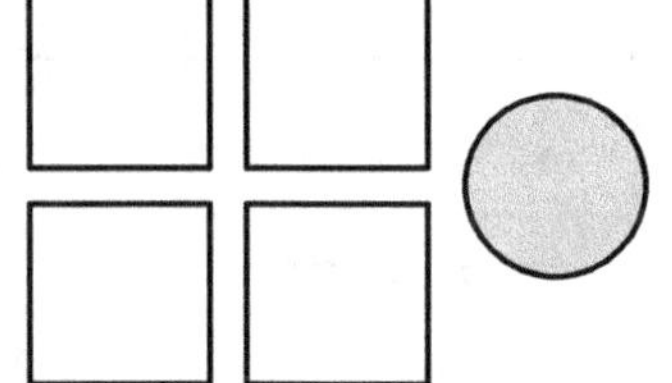 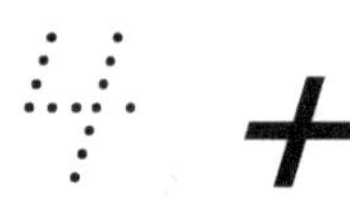

$4 + 1 = \underline{5}$

$6 + 1 = \underline{7}$

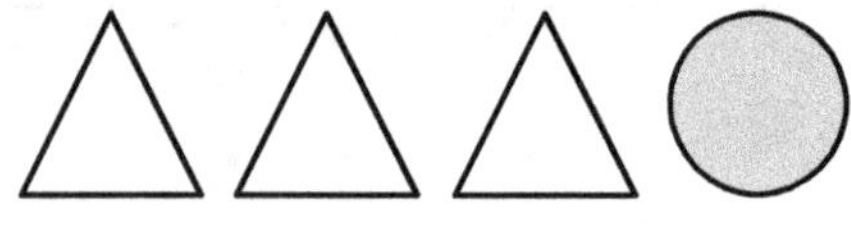

$3 + 1 = \underline{}$

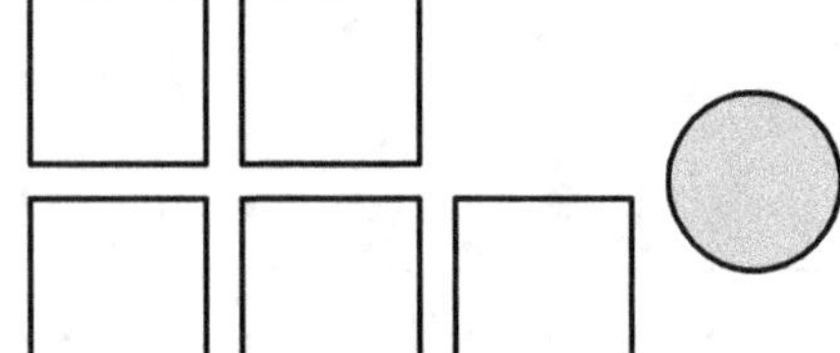

$5 + 1 = \underline{}$

Subtract a Spider

Trace the numbers and complete the subtraction problems below. Use the pictures to help.

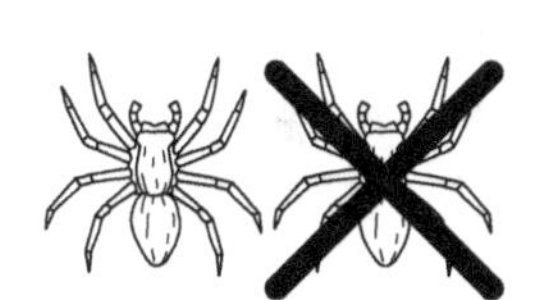

2 − 1 = 1

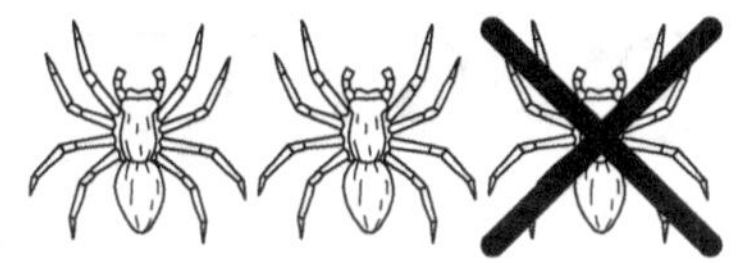

3 − 1 = 2

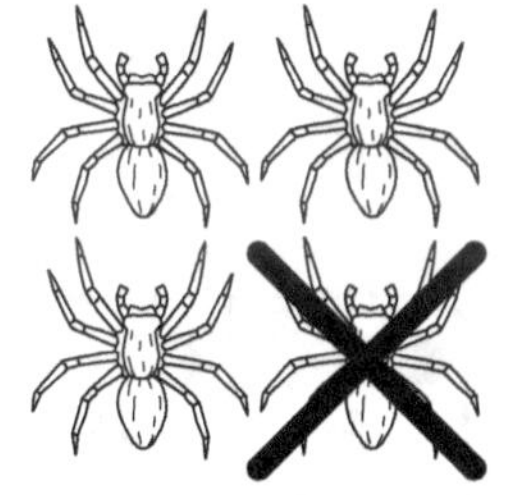

4 − 1 = ___

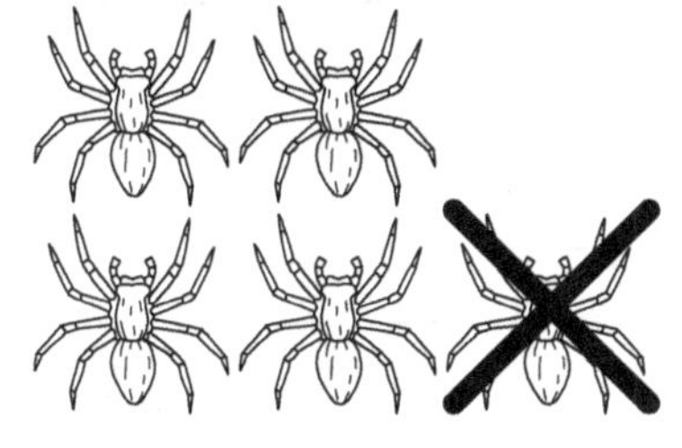

5 − 1 = ___

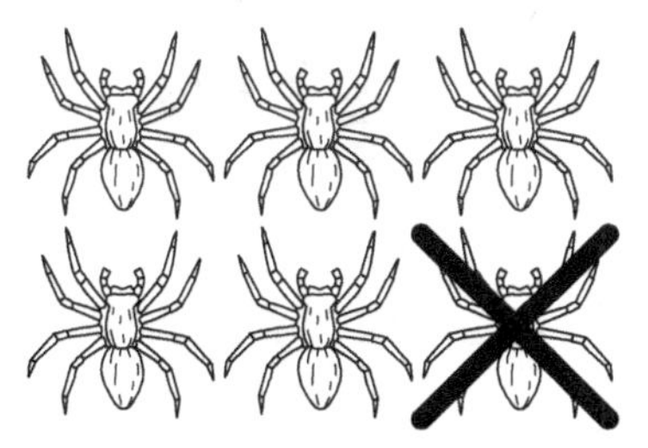

6 − 1 = ___

Which One Has More Dots?

Put an X on the domino that has more dots. Trace the numbers below.

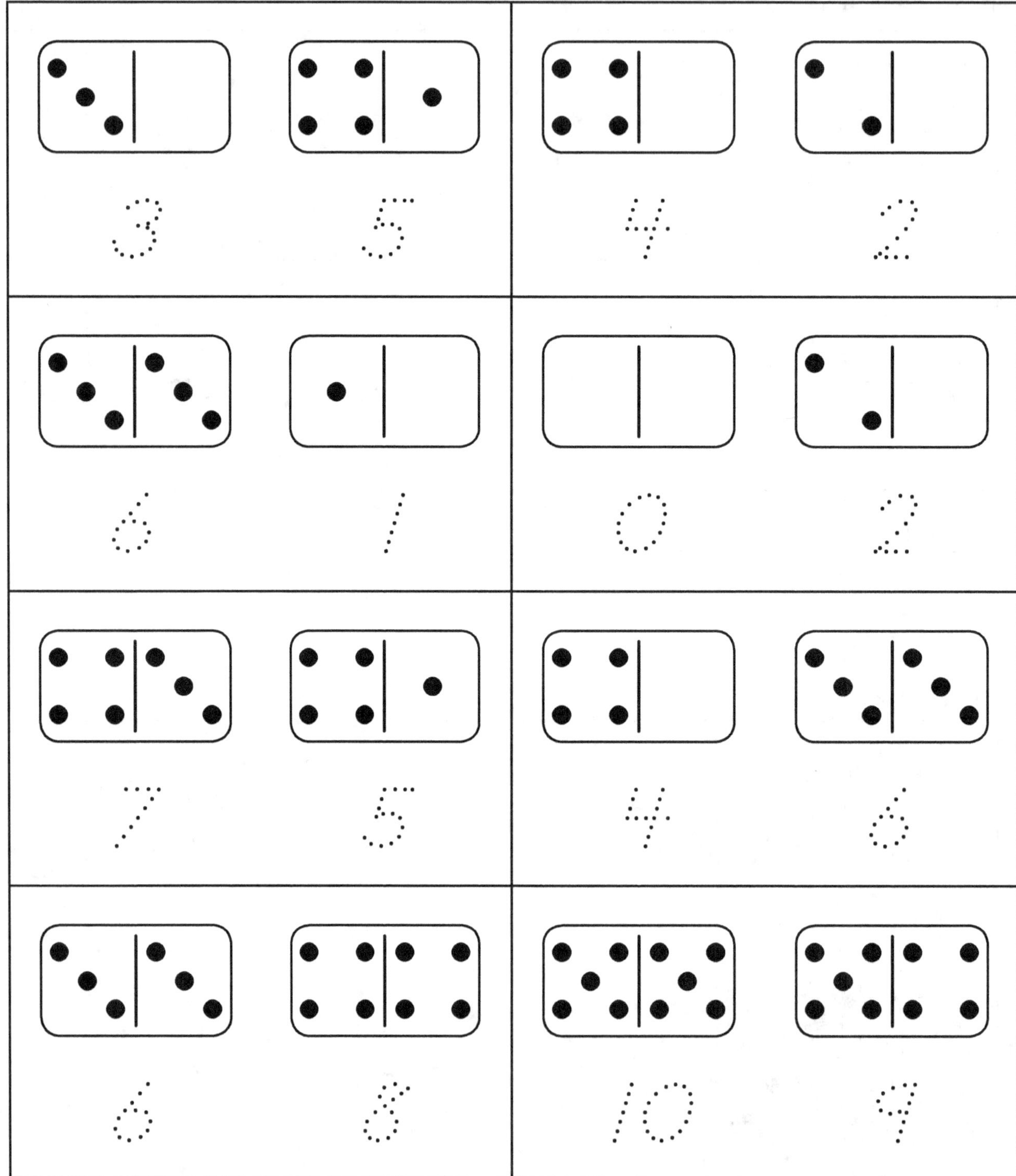

Put Them in Order

Use the numbers and dominoes to help with the problems below.

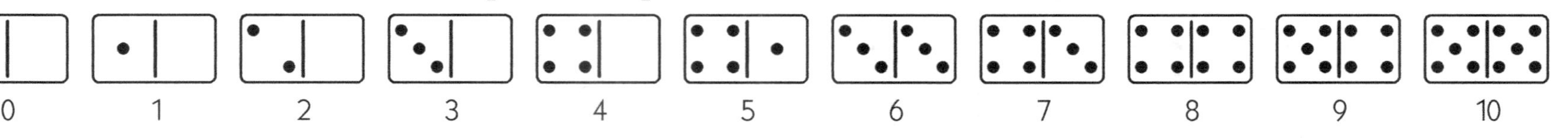

0   1   2   3   4   5   6   7   8   9   10

Trace the numbers. Then write them again in order from least to most.

5	6	4
4 ___	5 ___	6 ___

3	1	2
___	___	___

8	6	7
___	___	___

10	8	9
___	___	___

4	2	3
___	___	___

7	9	8
___	___	___

Comparing Cube Trains

1 Trace the numbers.

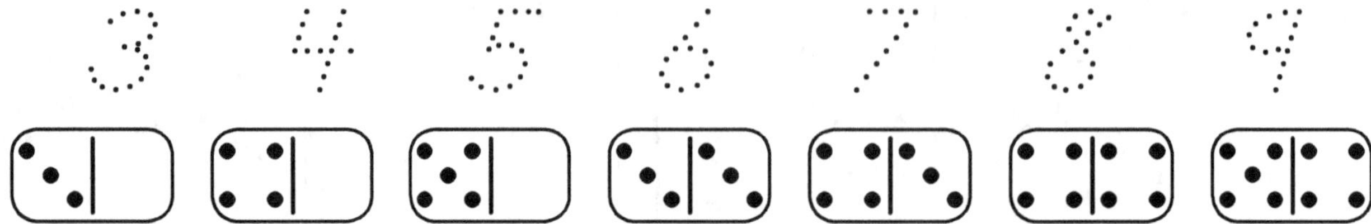

2 Count the cubes. Write the number to show how many. Draw an X on the train that is longer.

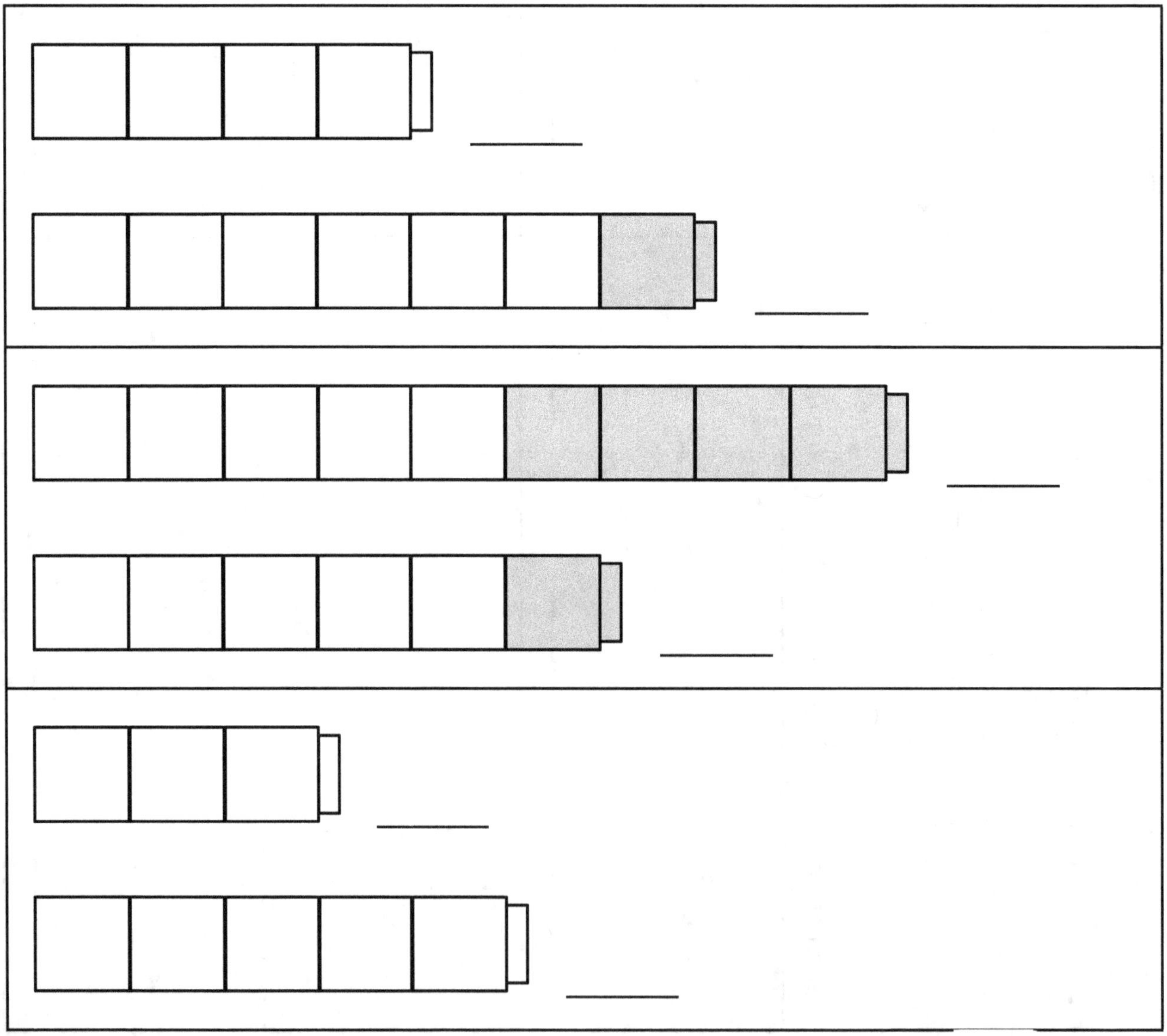

Which Is Longer? Which Is Shorter?

1 Draw a red X on the longer pencil. Color the shorter pencil green.

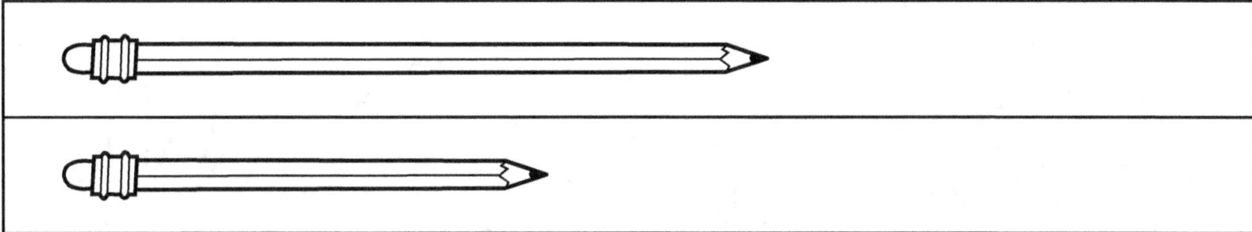

2 Color the longer vehicle yellow. Draw a circle around the shorter vehicle.

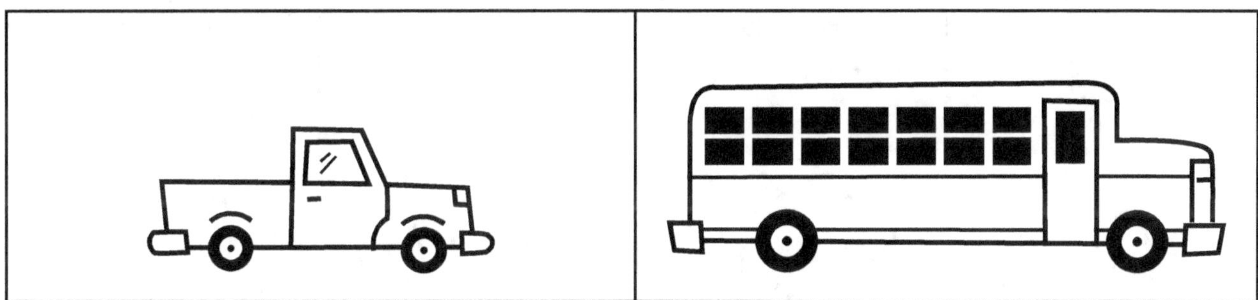

3 Color the longest ribbon blue. Color the shortest ribbon red.

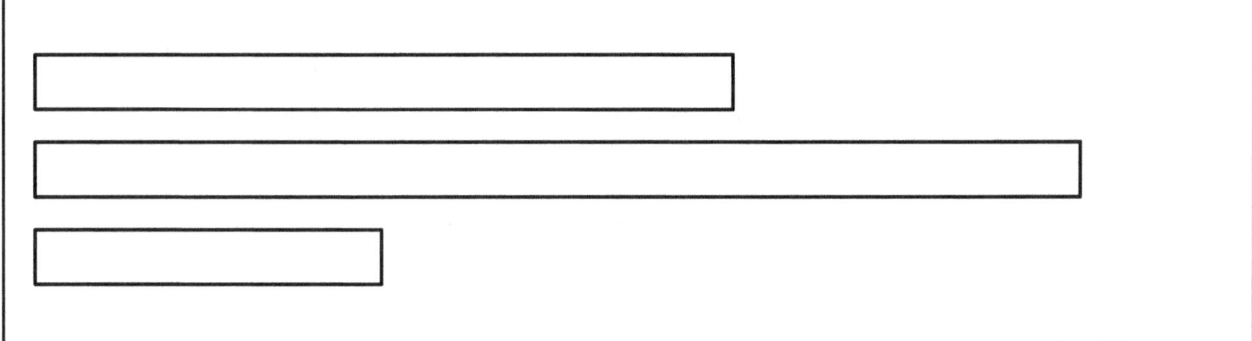

NAME _______________________________   **DATE** _______________________

Comparing Pennies: 0 1 2 3 4 5

1 How many pennies are there in each hand? Write the number to show. Draw a blue X on the hand with fewer pennies.

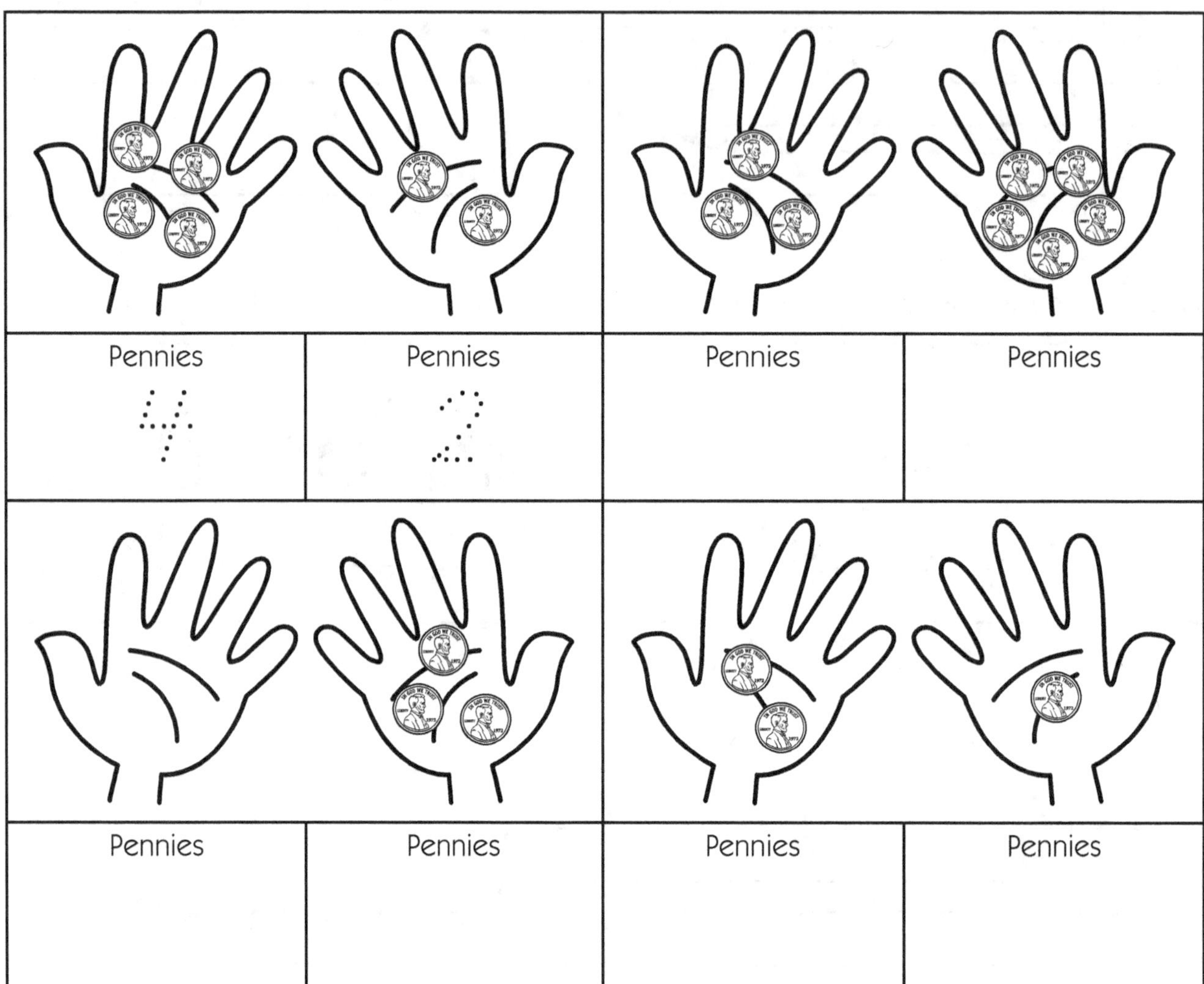

Pennies	Pennies	Pennies	Pennies
4	2		
Pennies	Pennies	Pennies	Pennies

2 Color the longest ribbon green. Color the shortest ribbon brown.

NAME _______________________ DATE _______________________

Count & Compare Pennies

Count the pennies in each frame. Write how many there are. Then draw lines to the words to show which frame has more and which frame has less.

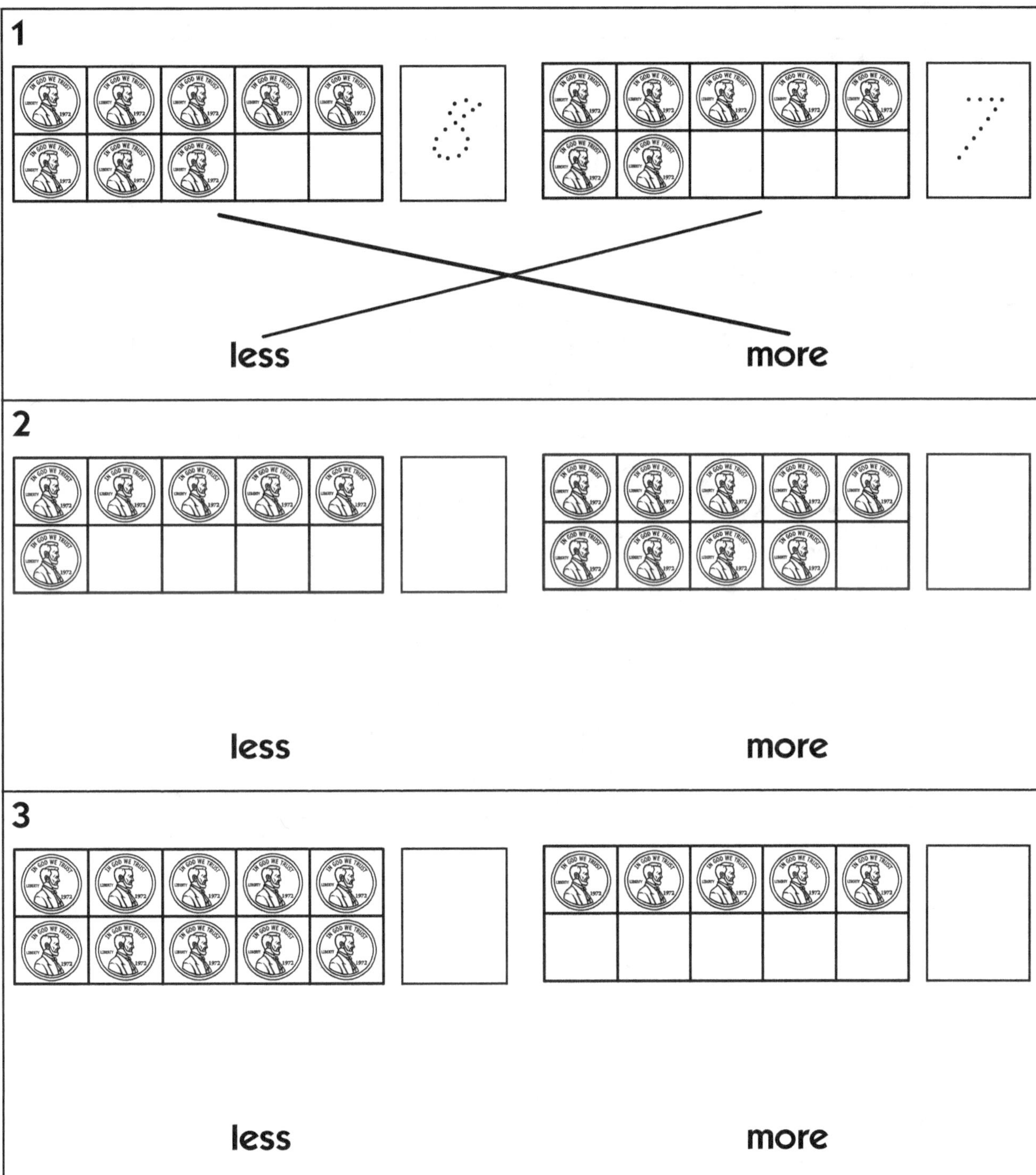

NAME _______________________________________ DATE _______________

A Growing Pattern of Ladybugs & Spots

1 Record the number of ladybugs and spots you see in each row.

How many ladybugs?		How many spots?
one		*2*
two		
three		
four		
five		
six		

2 Circle all of the counting by twos numbers:

1	(2)	3	(4)	5	(6)	7	8	9	10
11	12	13	14	15	16	17	18	19	20
21	22	23	24	25	26	27	28	29	30

NAME _______________________________   DATE _______________

Which Shapes Could It Be? Sheet 1

Circle all the shapes that fit the clues in each box.

1

Clues

____
straight sides

4 corners

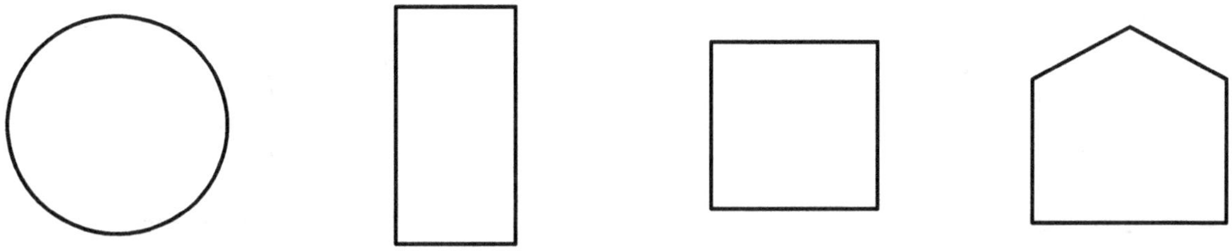

2

Clue

curved sides

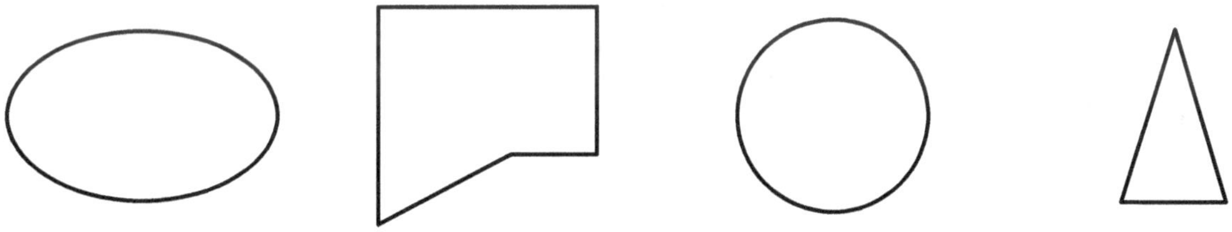

3

Clues

____
straight sides

3 corners

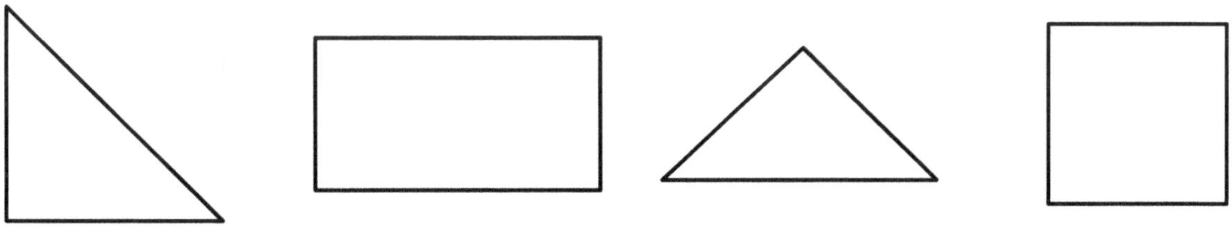

NAME ___________________________   DATE ___________________

Which Shapes Could It Be? Sheet 2

Color the shape that fits all the clues in each box.

1

Clues

______
straight sides   4 corners   small

2

Clues

curved sides   large

3

Clues

______
straight sides   3 corners   large

NAME _______________________ DATE _______________

Line Up Those Numbers

1 Trace each number. Then write it again in the box below.

0	1	2	3	4	5	6	7	8	9

2 Fill in the missing numbers on the number lines below.

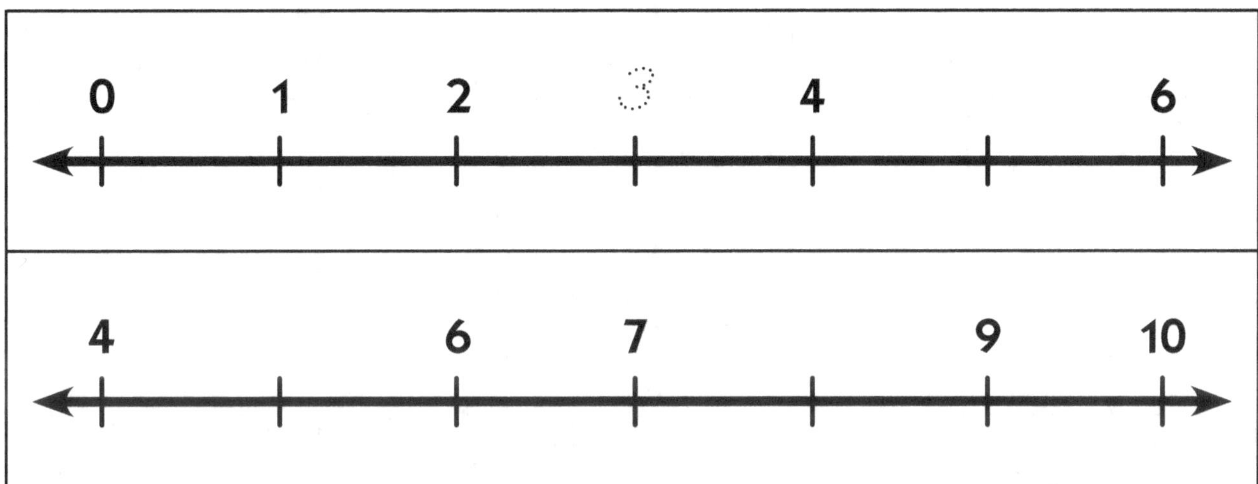

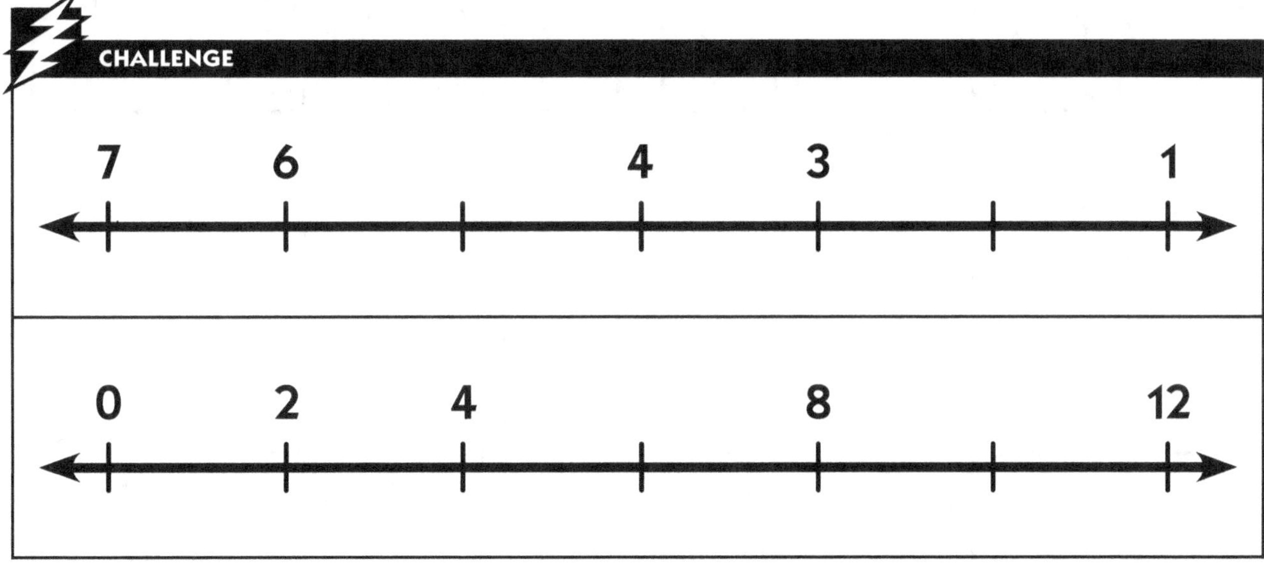

Coloring Cubes 5–10

Color in the cubes below.

Color 9 cubes.	Color 7 cubes.	Color 5 cubes.
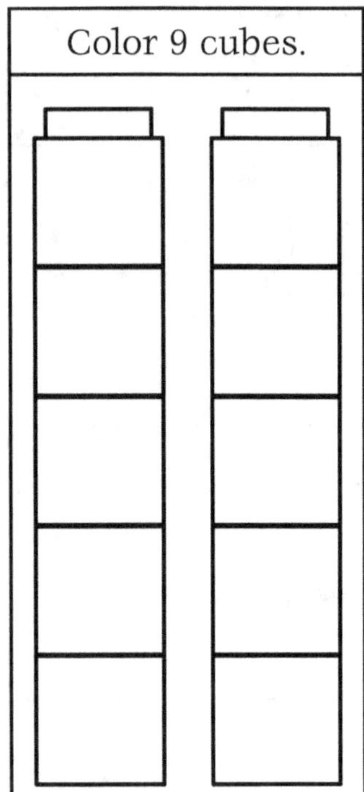	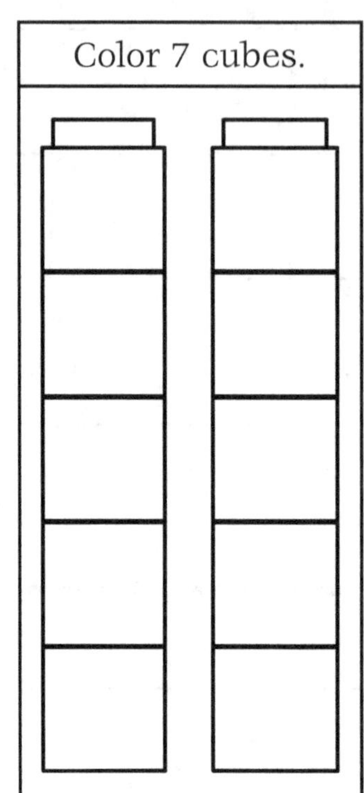	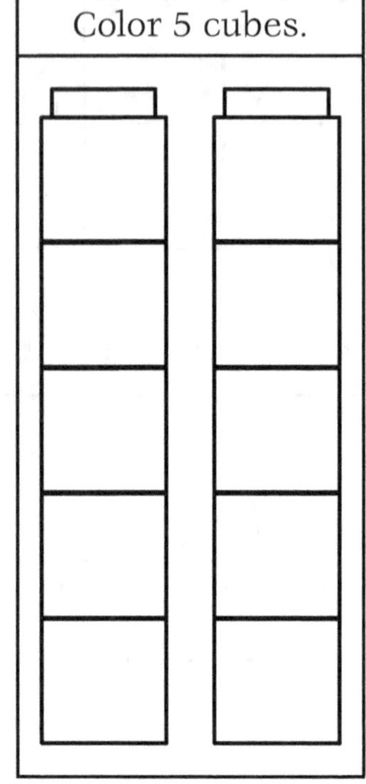

Color 8 cubes.	Color 10 cubes.	Color 6 cubes.
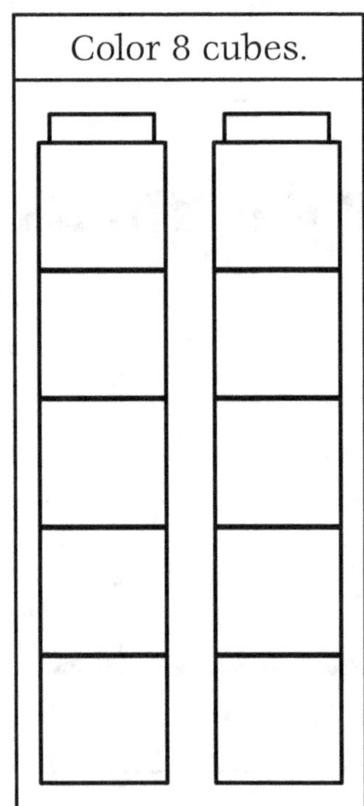	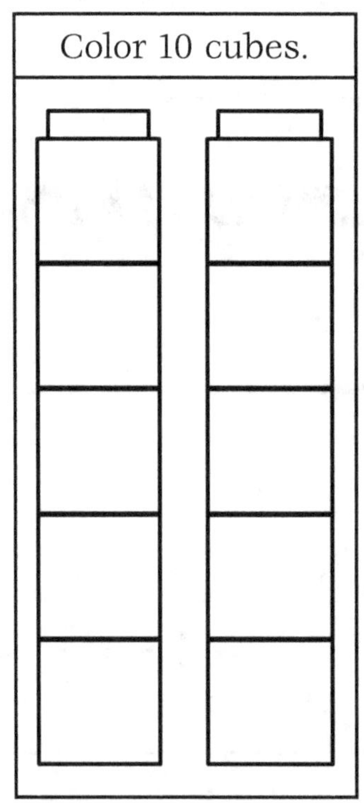	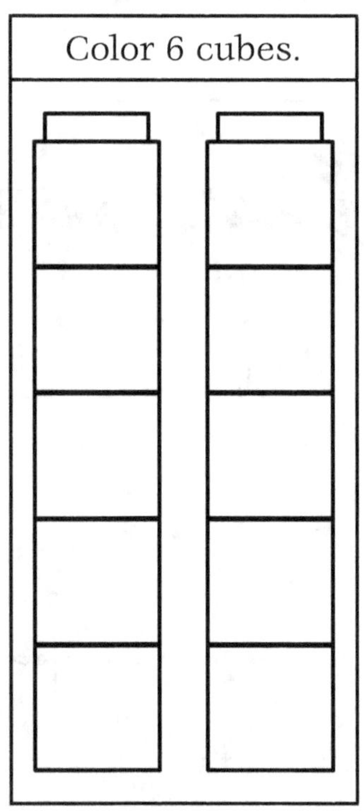

Dots 11–15

Count the dots in each double ten frame. Trace the numbers.

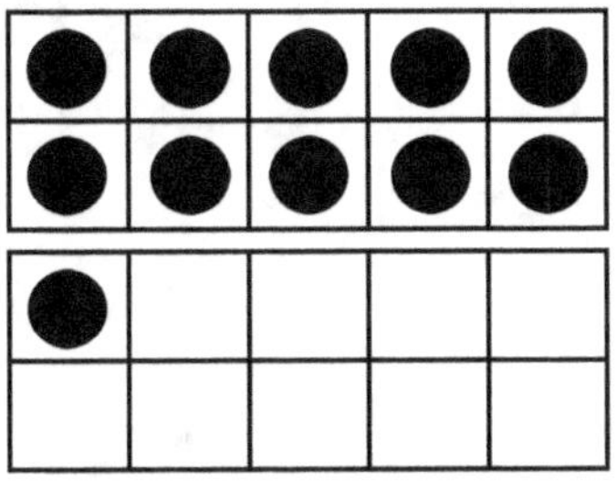

11   11   11

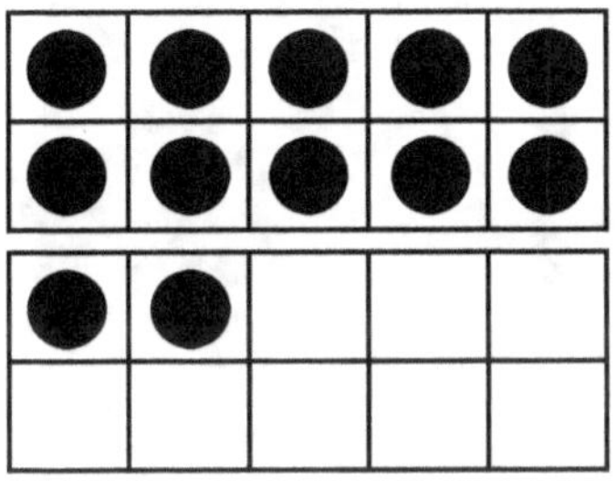

12   12   12

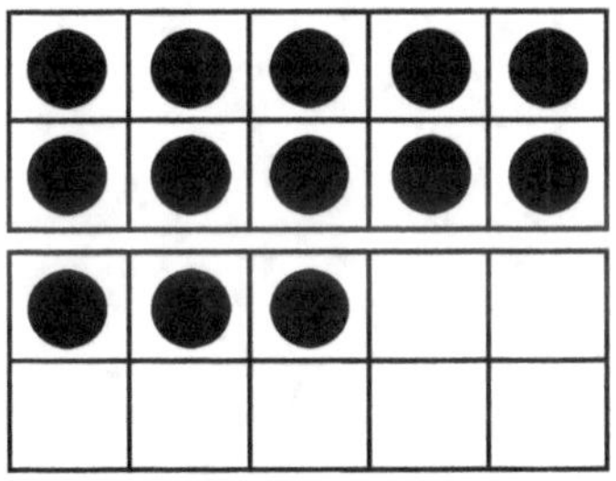

13   13   13

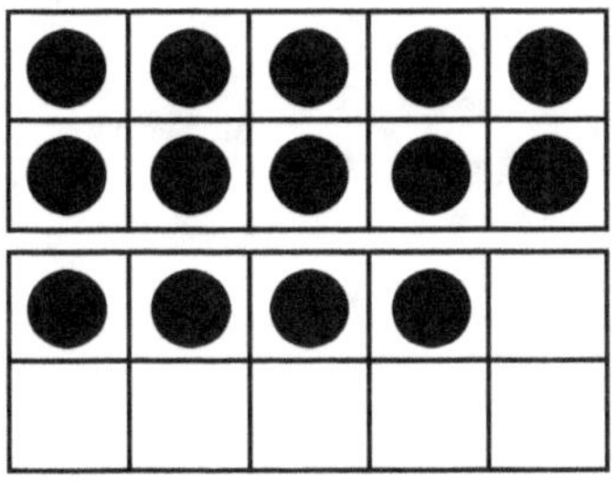

14   14   14

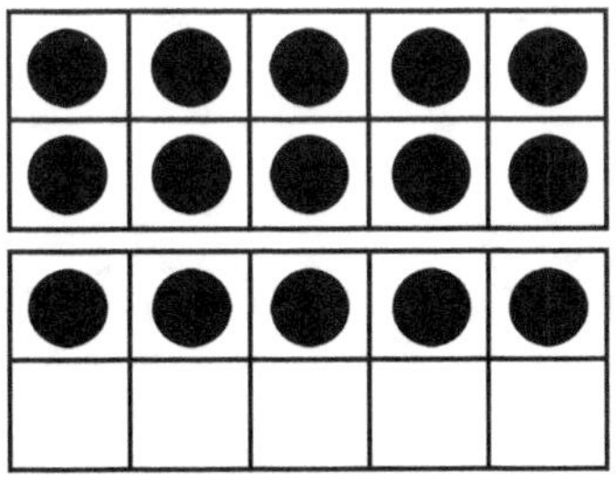

15   15   15

NAME ______________________ DATE ______________

Dots 16–20

Count the dots in each double ten frame. Trace the numbers.

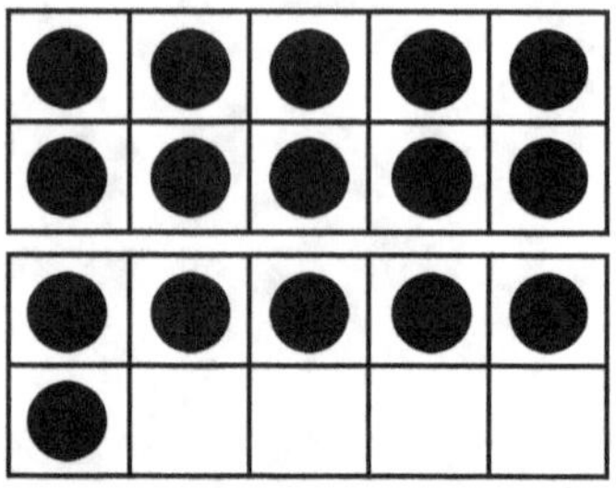

16 16 16

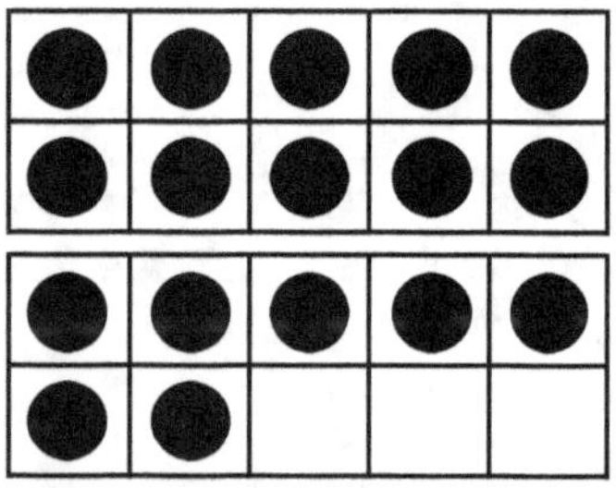

17 17 17

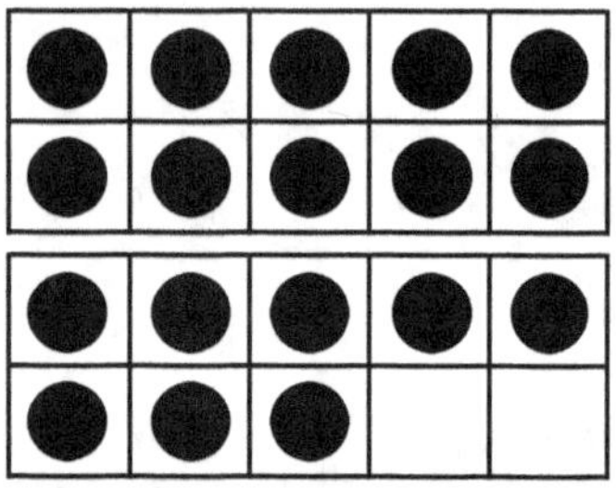

18 18 18

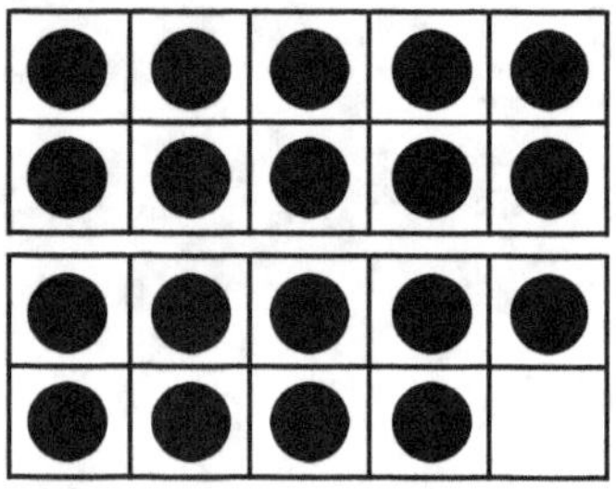

19 19 19

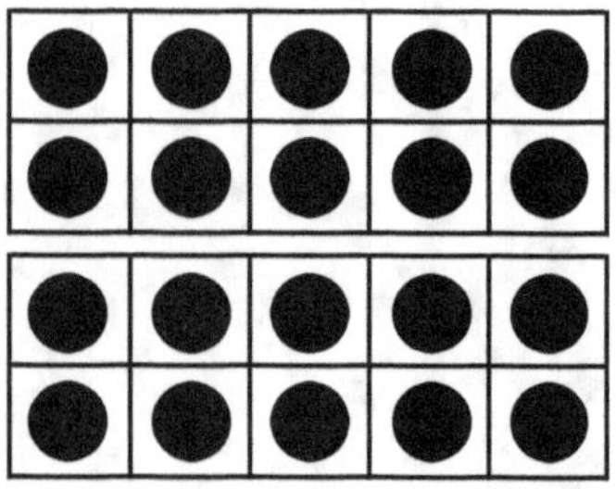

20 20 20

Count the Dots

1 Trace each number.

15　　16　　17　　18　　19　　20

2 Count the number of dots in each set of double ten frames and record the number.

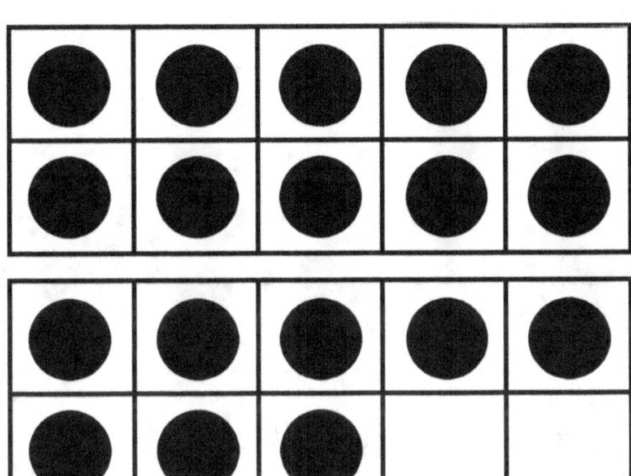

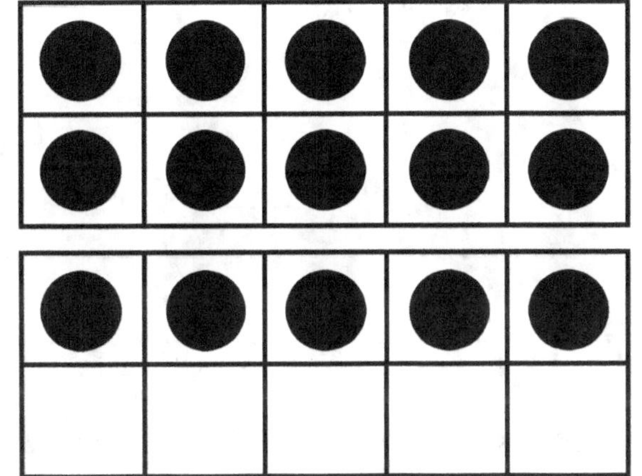

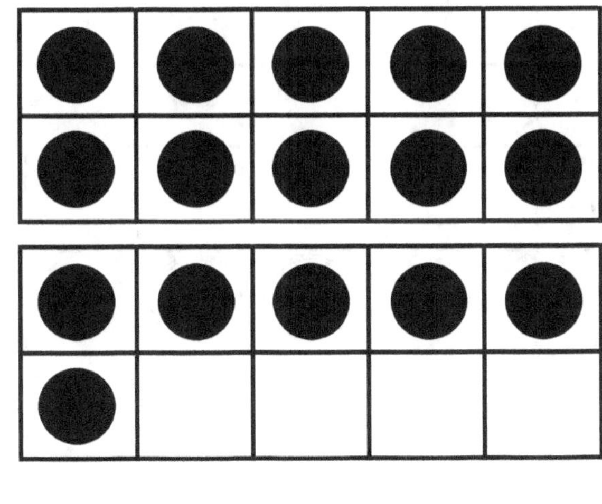

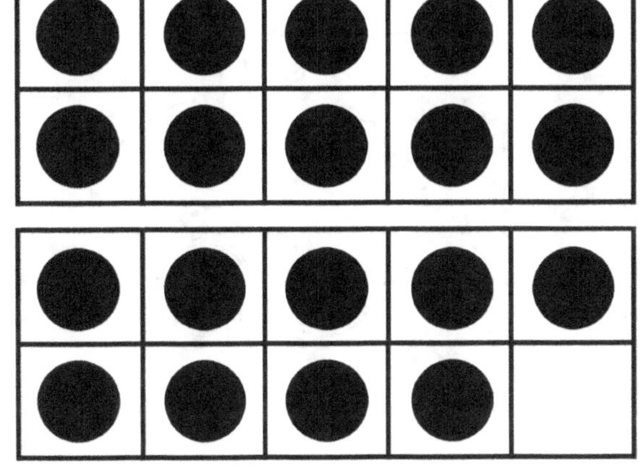

Add the Pennies

Solve the addition problems. Use the pictures to help.

$$2¢ + 3¢ = \text{\_\_\_\_\_\_} ¢$$

$$3¢ + 2¢ = \text{\_\_\_\_\_\_} ¢$$

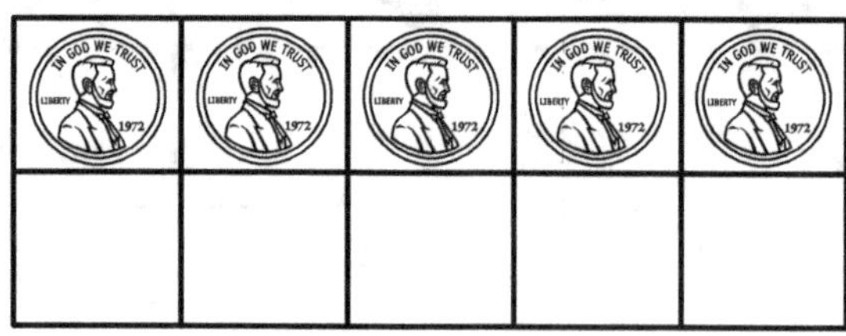

$$5¢ + 0¢ = \text{\_\_\_\_\_\_} ¢$$

$$4¢ + 1¢ = \text{\_\_\_\_\_\_} ¢$$

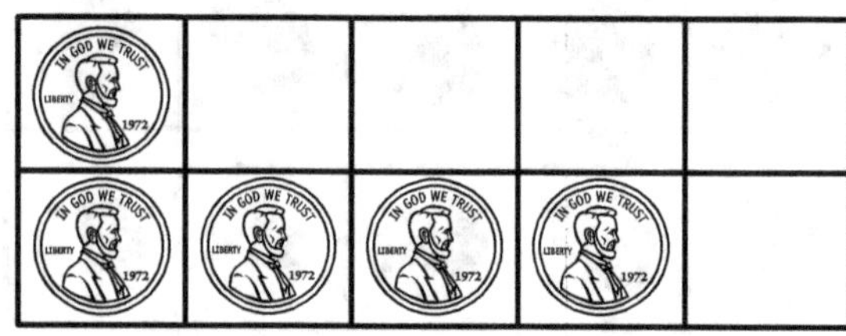

$$1¢ + 4¢ = \text{\_\_\_\_\_\_} ¢$$

$$0¢ + 5¢ = \text{\_\_\_\_\_\_} ¢$$

Make 4

1 Color the cubes to match each equation.

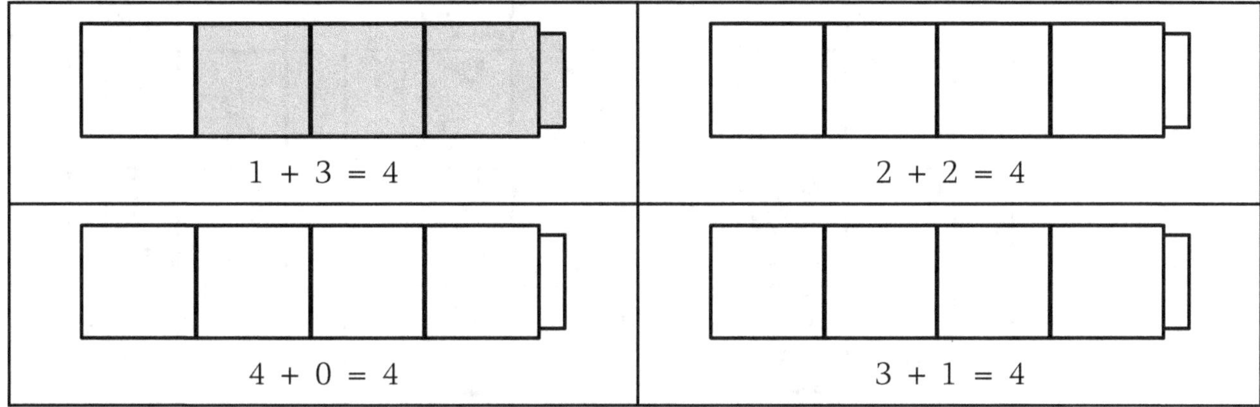

$1 + 3 = 4$

$2 + 2 = 4$

$4 + 0 = 4$

$3 + 1 = 4$

2 Trace the numbers and solve the problems. Use the pictures to help.

$3 + 1 = \underline{}$

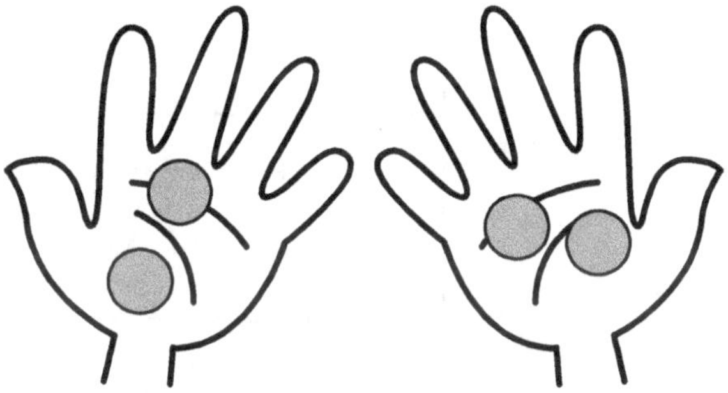

$2 + 2 = \underline{}$

$0 + 4 = \underline{}$

$\underline{} + \underline{} = 4$

NAME ___________________   DATE ___________________

How Many Insects? Add Them Up

Solve the addition problems. Use the pictures to help.

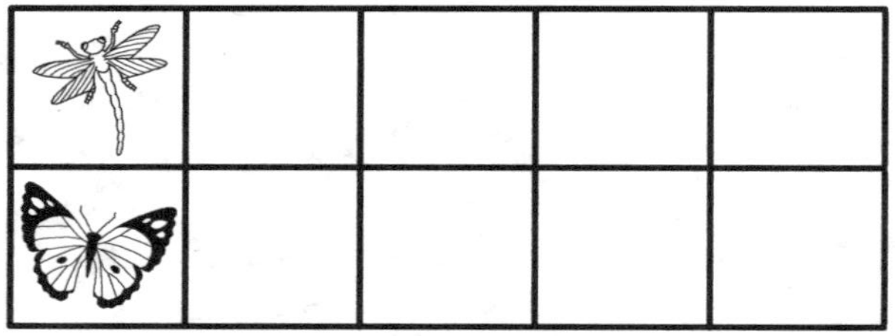

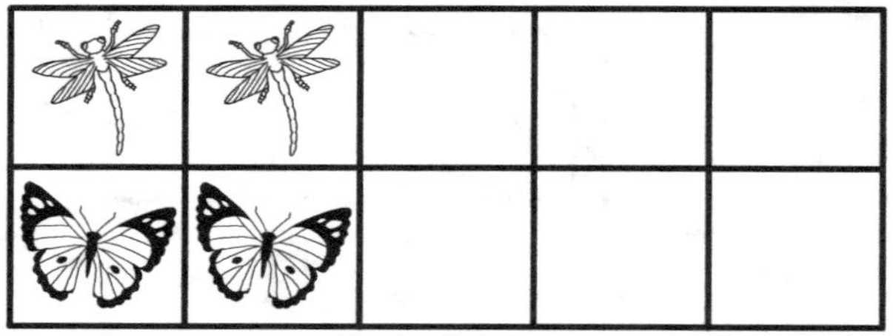

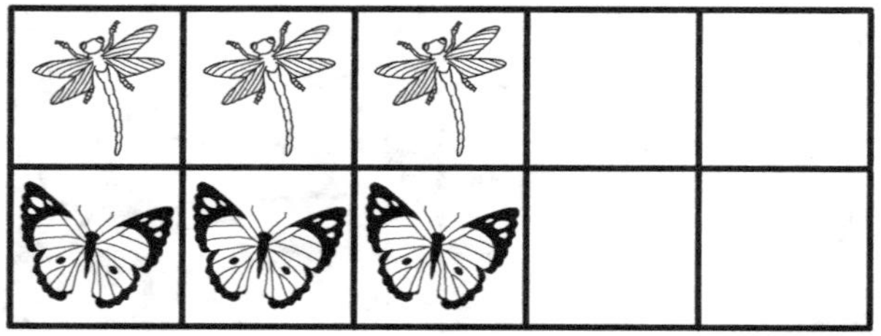

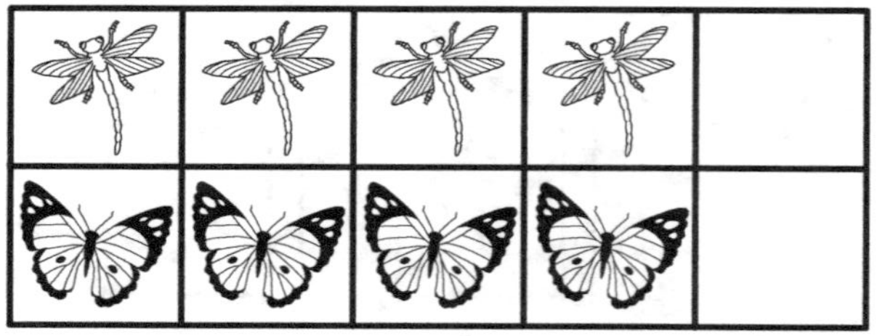

1 + 1 = 2		2 + 2 =
3 + 3 =		4 + 4 =
4 + 4 =		5 + 5 =

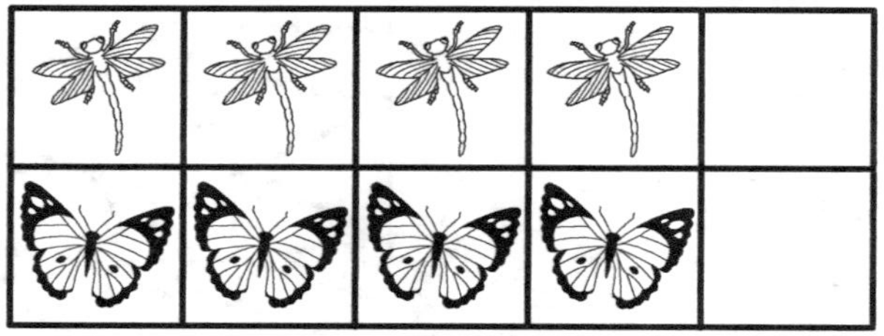

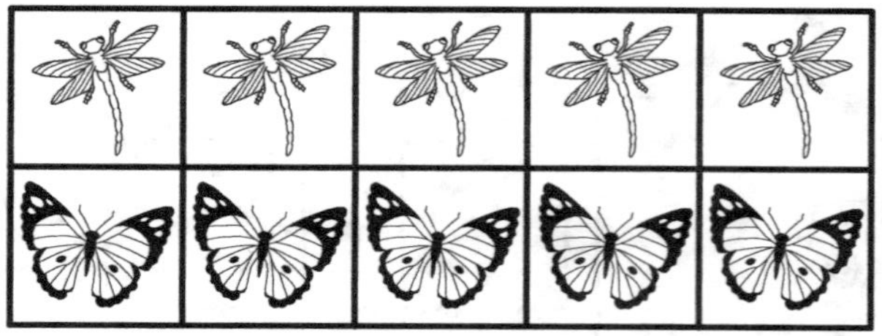

A Story Problem

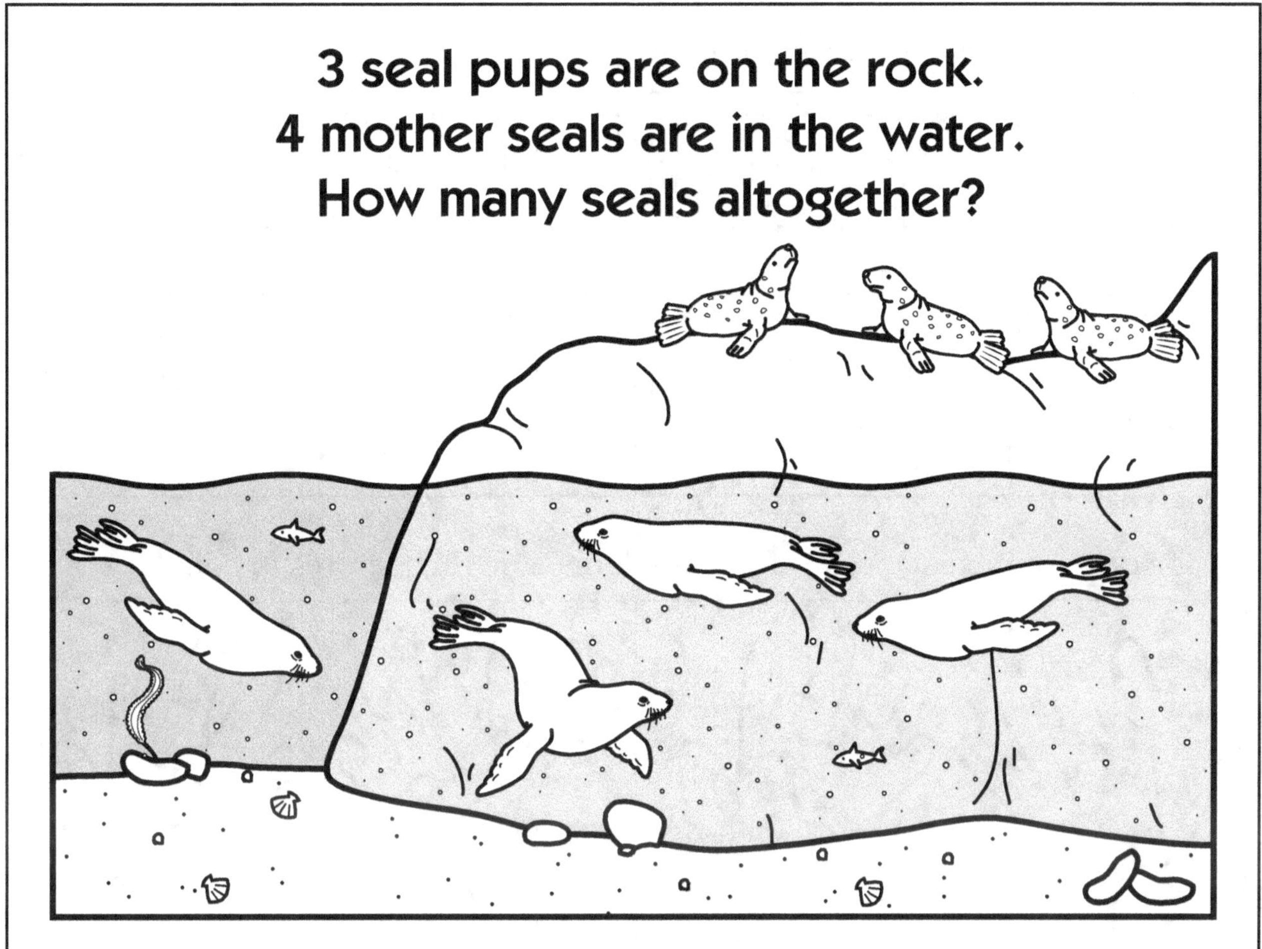

Use pictures and numbers to show how you solve the problem.

Make 5

1 Color the cubes to match each equation.

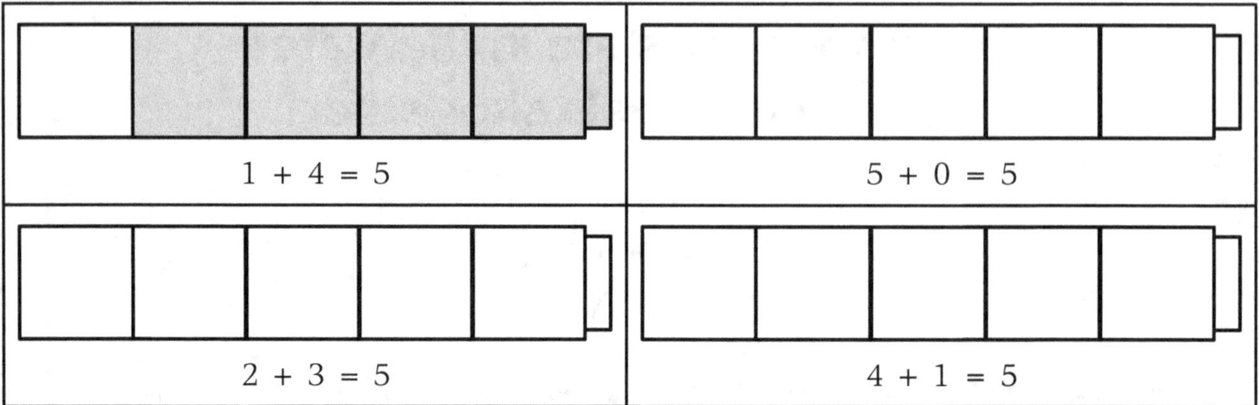

$1 + 4 = 5$

$5 + 0 = 5$

$2 + 3 = 5$

$4 + 1 = 5$

2 Trace the numbers and solve the problems. Use the pictures to help.

$3 + 2 = \underline{\hspace{1cm}}$

$4 + 1 = \underline{\hspace{1cm}}$

$0 + 5 = \underline{\hspace{1cm}}$

$\underline{\hspace{1cm}} + \underline{\hspace{1cm}} = 5$

Counting Dimes

Use the following information to help solve the problems below.

10¢
1 dime

1 Trace the numbers.

2 How many cents? Write the amount.

(1 dime)	_10_ ¢
(2 dimes)	_____ ¢
(3 dimes)	_____ ¢
(4 dimes)	_____ ¢
(5 dimes)	_____ ¢

Make 6

1 Color the cubes to match each equation.

$1 + 5 = 6$

$2 + 4 = 6$

$3 + 3 = 6$

$6 + 0 = 6$

2 Trace the numbers and solve the problems. Use the pictures to help.

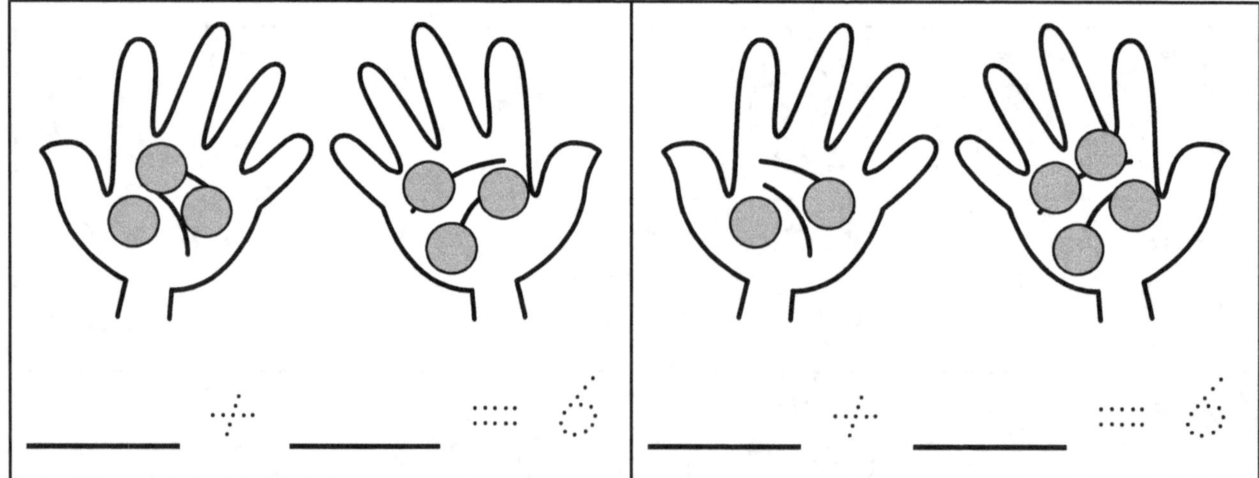

Hot or Cold Weather?

1 Circle each picture that shows hot weather. Put a line under each picture that shows cold weather.

2 Draw a picture to go with the descriptions below.

Here is something I like to do when it's hot outside.	Here is something I like to do when it's cold outside.

Count the Cubes

1 Trace each number.

10   11   12   13   14   15

2 Count the cubes in each set and record the number.

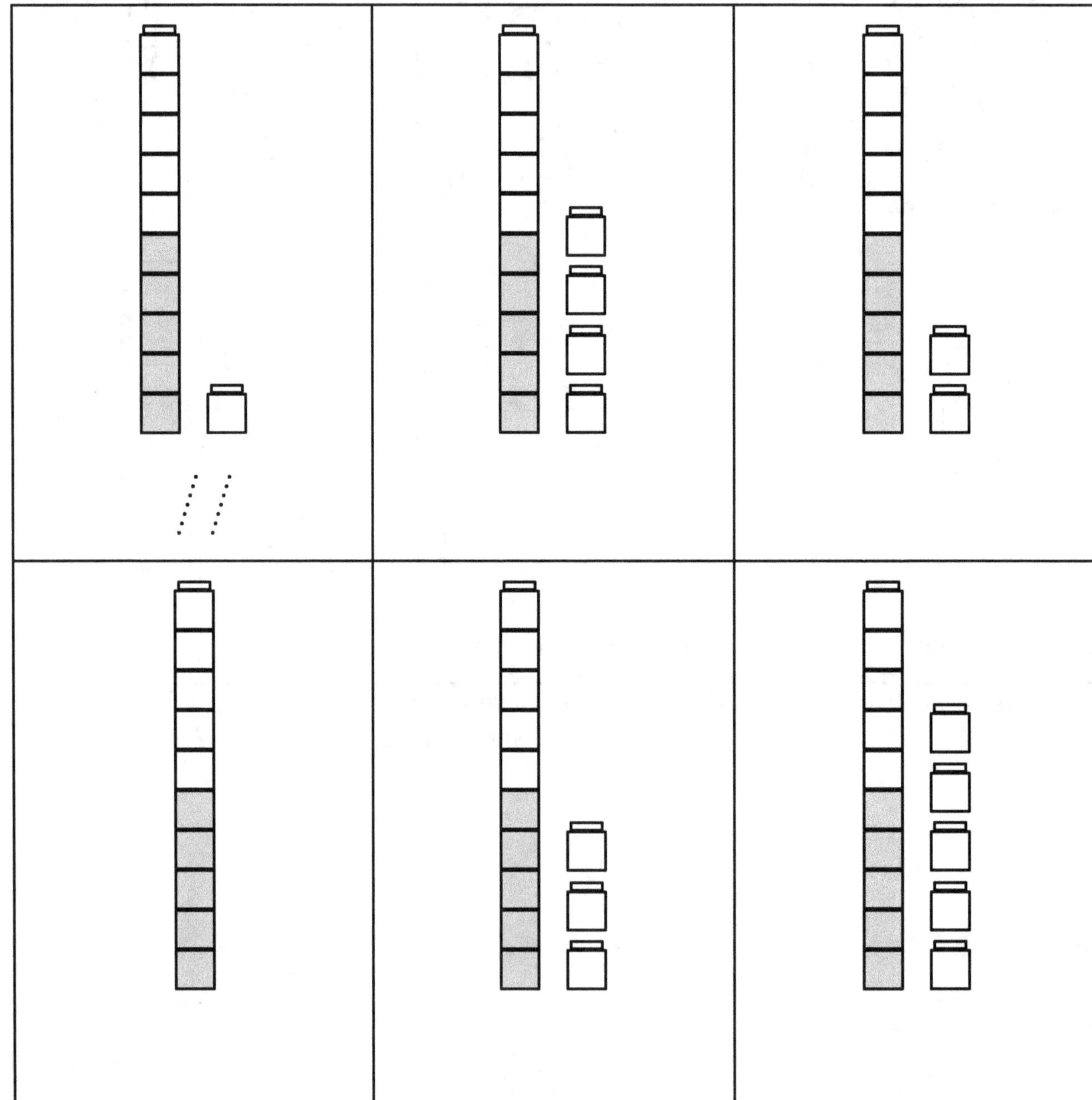

Tens & Ones How Many?

How many cubes in each set? Write the number to show.

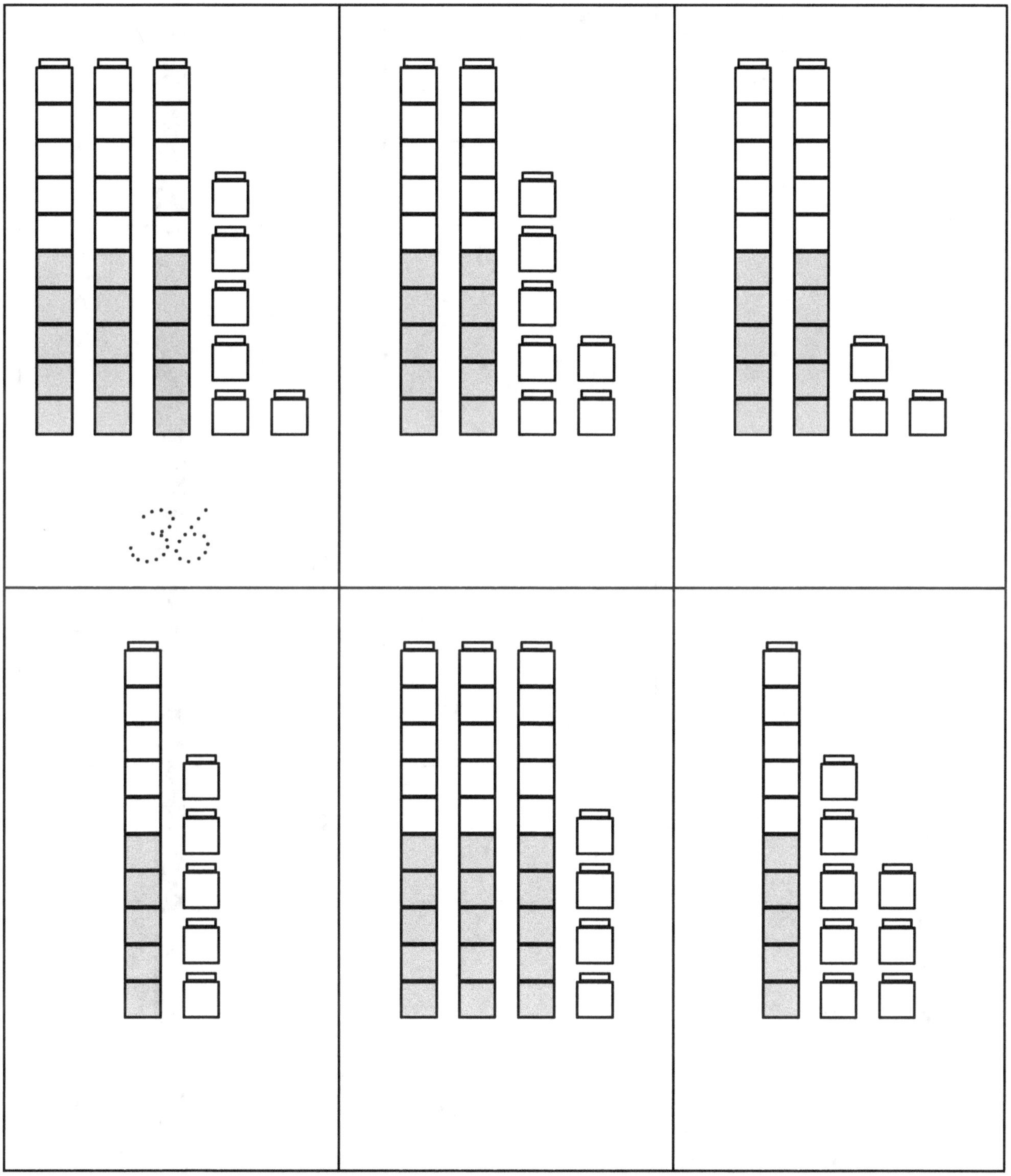

NAME __________________________ DATE __________________________

What's Missing? Sheet 1

1 Trace each number.

1 2 3 4 5 6 7 8 9 10

2 Fill in the mising numbers.

1	2	3		5	6	7		9	10
11	12		14	15		17	18		20
21		23		25	26			29	30

CHALLENGE

31				35		37			40

What's Missing? Sheet 2

1 Fill in the missing numbers on this calendar.

Sunday	Monday	Tuesday	Wednesday	Thursday	Friday	Saturday
				1	2	3
4		6	7	8		10
11	12		14		16	17
18		20	21		23	
25		27		29		31

2 How many days are there in a week?

Calendar Markers

1 The shapes on the calendar form a repeating pattern but some are missing. Fill them in.

Sunday	Monday	Tuesday	Wednesday	Thursday	Friday	Saturday
	○ 1	▭ 2	▭ 3	○ 4	▭ 5	▭ 6
○ 7	▭ 8	▭ 9	○ 10	▭ 11	▭ 12	13
▭ 14	15	16	▭ 17	▭ 18	19	▭ 20
▭ 21	○ 22	▭ 23	24	○ 25	26	▭ 27
○ 28	29	▭ 30	31			

2 How many days are there in a week?

Cats & Dogs Addition

Fill in the numbers and then solve the addition problem. Use the pictures to help.

1

_______ Cats   +   _______ Dogs   =   _______

2

_______ Cats   +   _______ Dog   =   _______

3

_______ Cats   +   _______ Dogs   =   _______

Frog & Toad Probability

1 Frog got 6 spins. Toad got 4 spins. Color the graph to show.

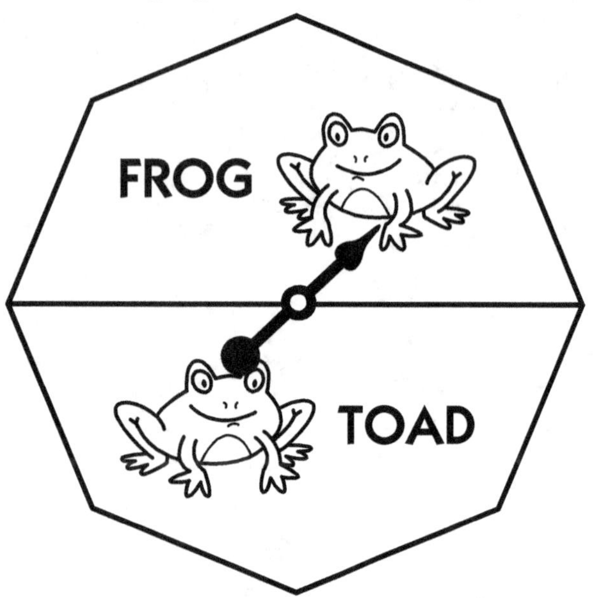

2 How many more spins did Frog get than Toad?

3 How many spins did Frog and Toad get in all?

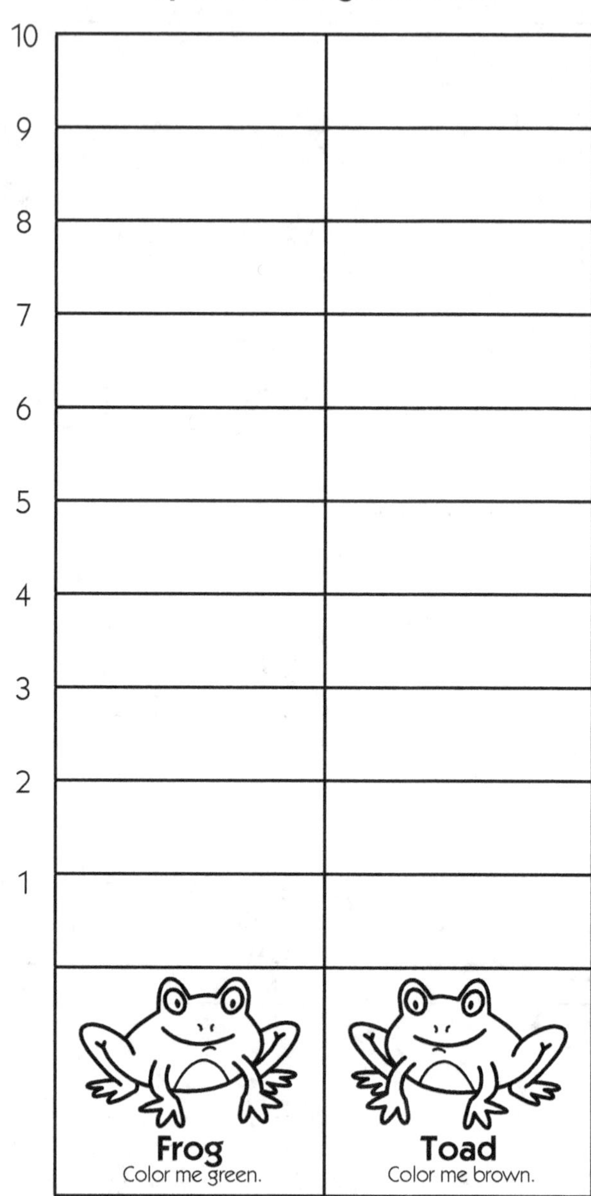

What Time Is It?

Draw lines to connect the clocks and time cards.

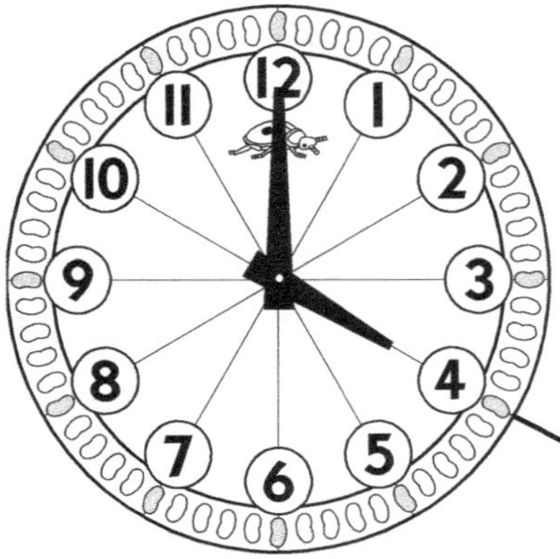

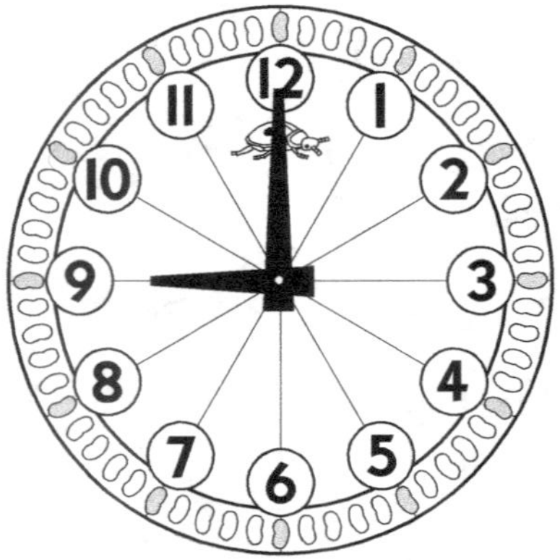

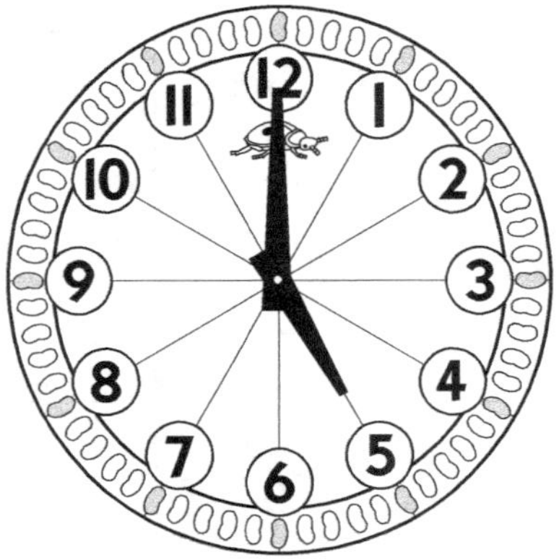

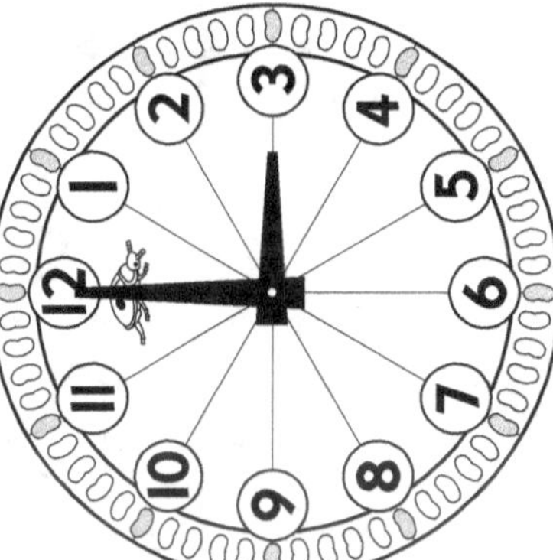

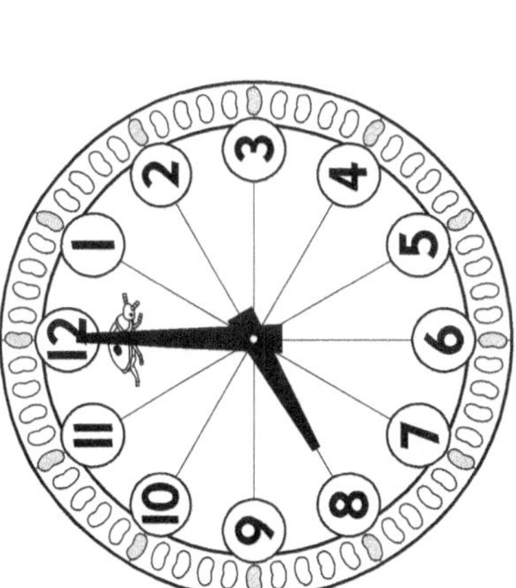

1:00	3:00	5:00	4:00	8:00	9:00
one o'clock	three o'clock	five o'clock	four o'clock	eight o'clock	nine o'clock

More about 4

Trace the numbers. Fill in the missing numbers to complete the equations. Use the pictures to help.

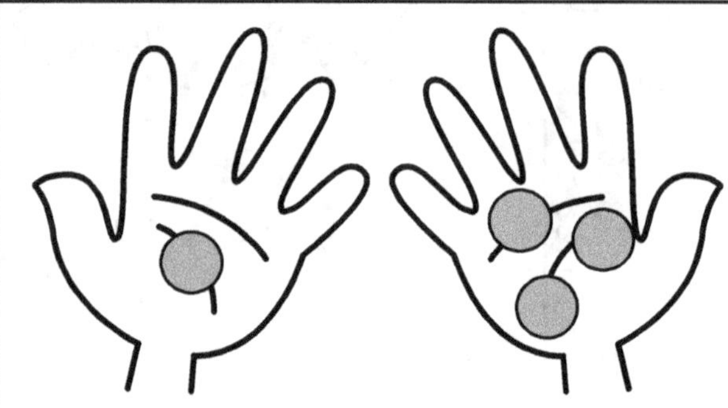

___ + ___ = 4

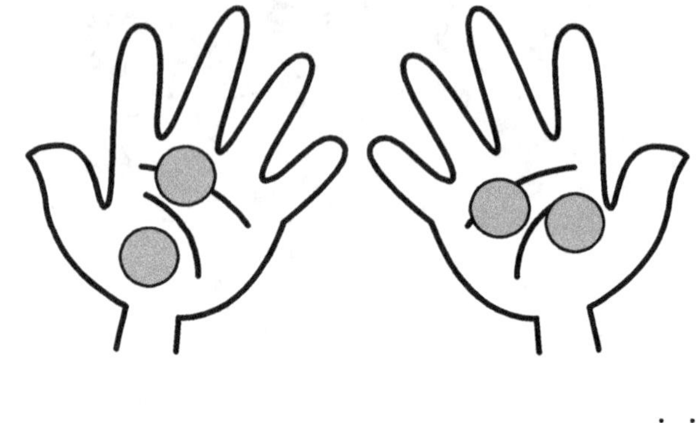

___ + ___ = 4

3 + ___ = 4

2 + ___ = 4

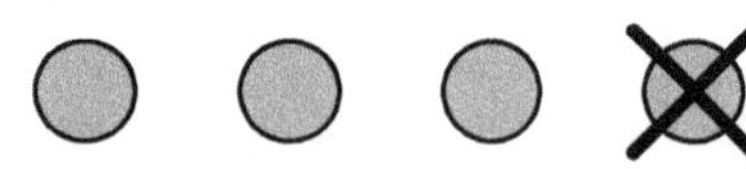

4 − 1 = 3

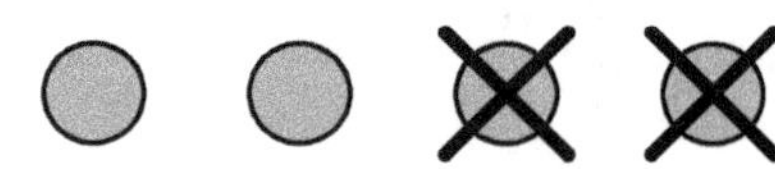

4 − 2 = 2

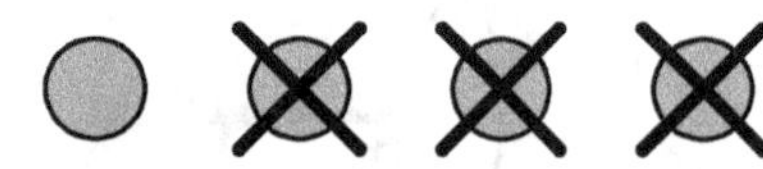

4 − 3 = 1

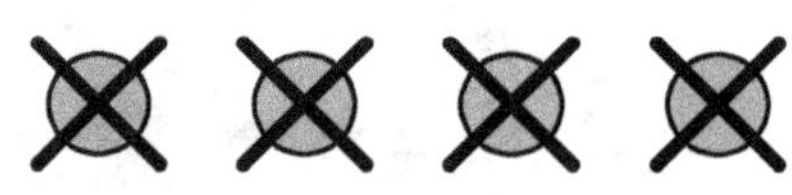

4 − 4 = 0

What's Missing? Sheet 3

Fill in the missing numbers. Use the pictures to help.

_______¢ + 3¢ = 5¢

_______¢ + 2¢ = 5¢

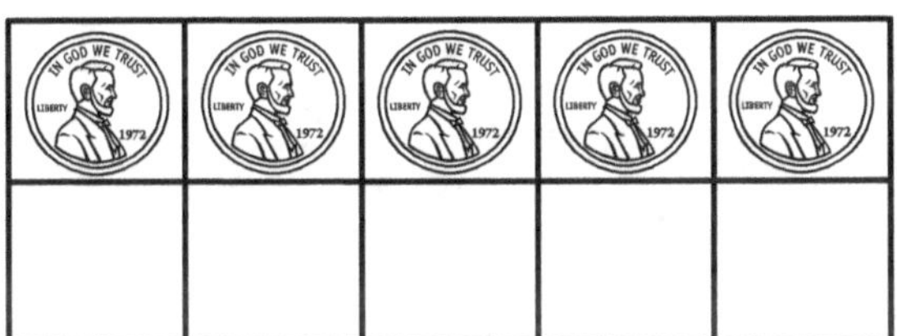

_______¢ + 0¢ = 5¢

_______¢ + 1¢ = 5¢

_______¢ + 4¢ = 5¢

_______¢ + 5¢ = 5¢

Frog Story Problem

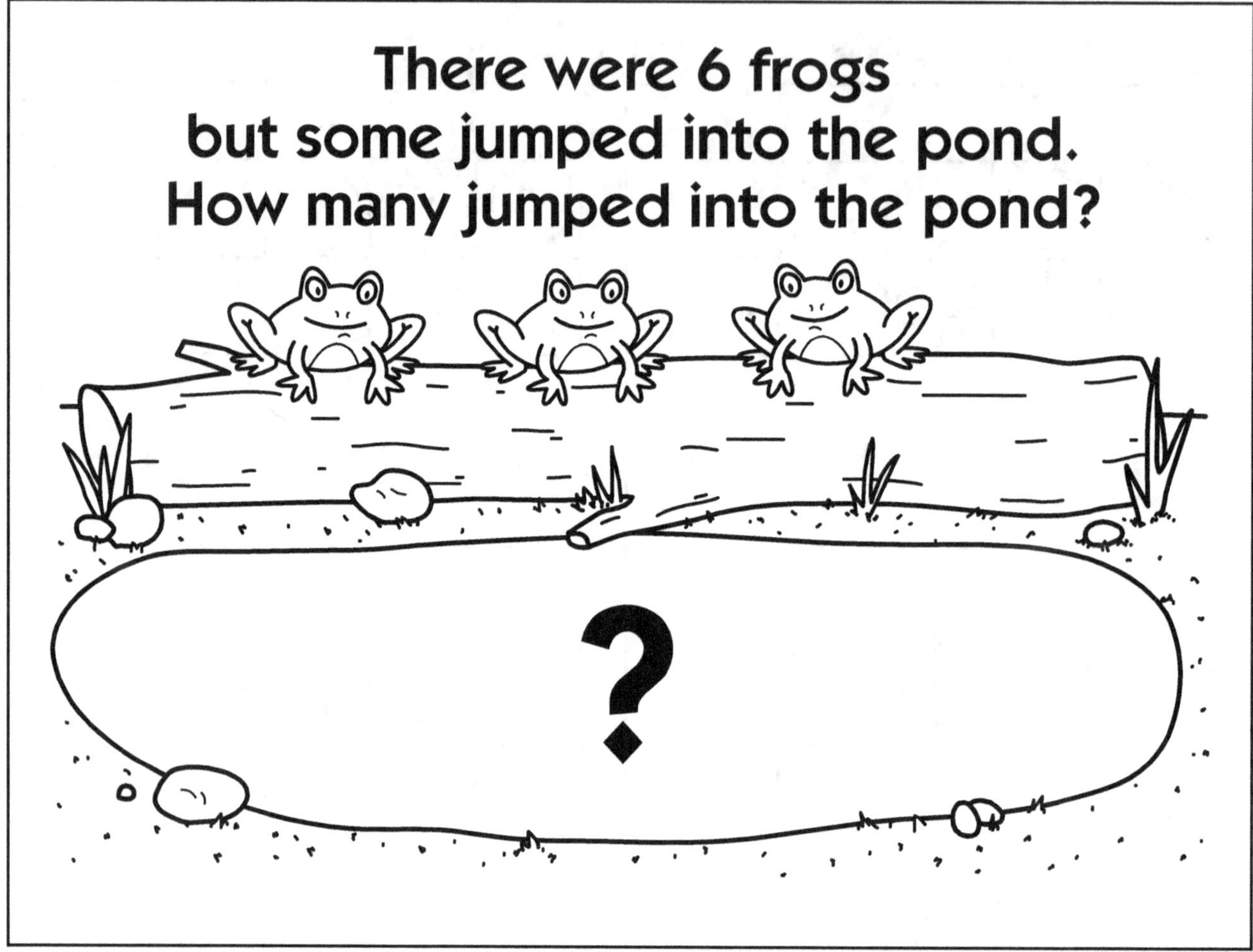

Use pictures and numbers to show how you solve the problem.

More Frog Problems

Use pictures and numbers to show how you solve each problem.

Counting By Fives Sheet 1

1 Trace each number.

5   10   15   20   25   30

2 How many cubes in each set? Write the numbers.

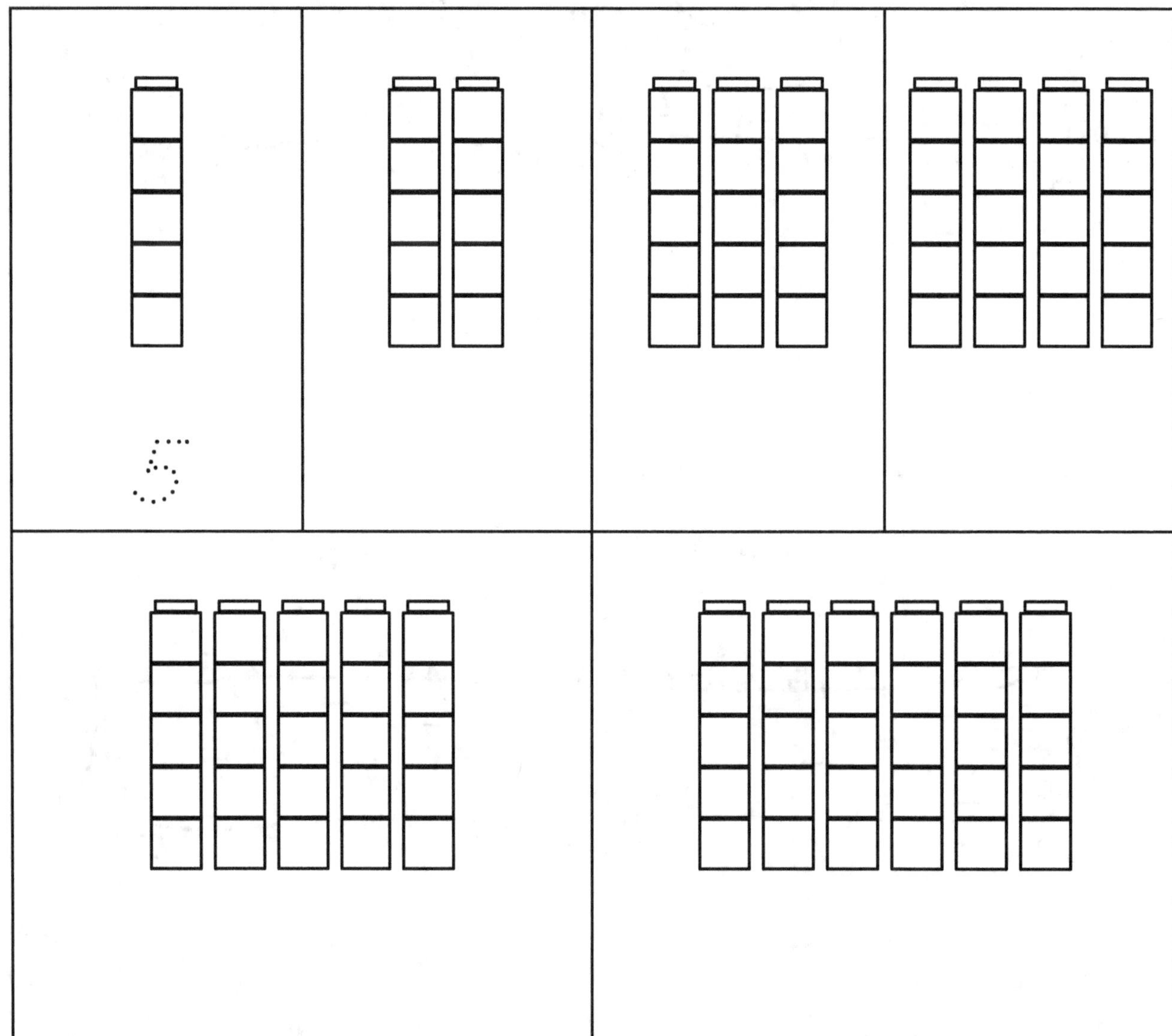

Counting Nickels

Use the following information to help solve the problems below.

5¢
1 nickel

1 Trace each number.

5   10   15   20   25   30

2 How many cents? Write the amount.

	 5 ¢
 	 _____ ¢
  	 _____ ¢
   	 _____ ¢
    	_____ ¢

More about 5

Trace the numbers. Fill in the missing numbers to complete the equations.

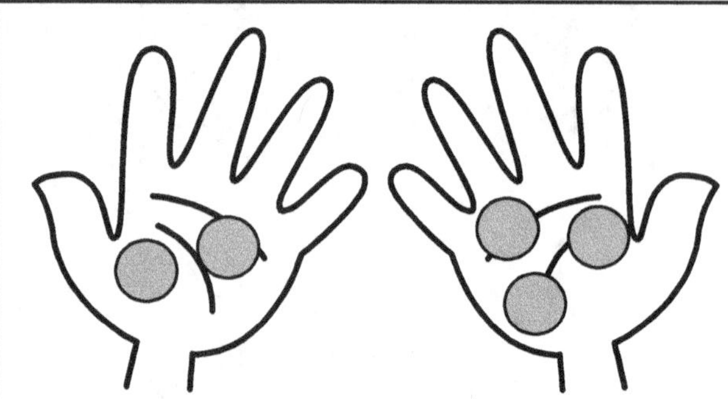

___ + ___ = 5

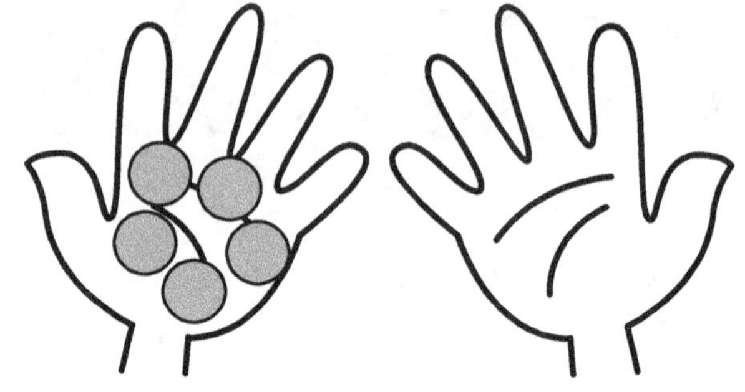

___ + ___ = 5

3 + ___ = 5

2 + ___ = 5

5 − 1 = 4

5 − 2 = 3

5 − 3 = 2

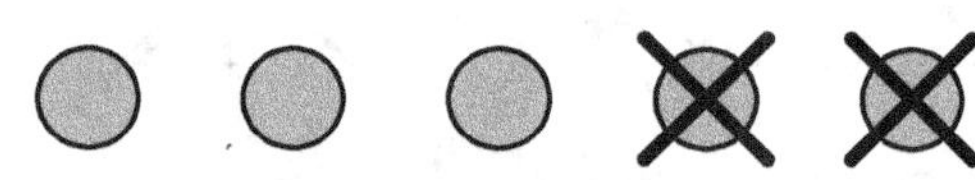

5 − 4 = 1

Counting By Fives Sheet 2

1 Trace each number.

2 How many cubes in each set? Write the numbers.

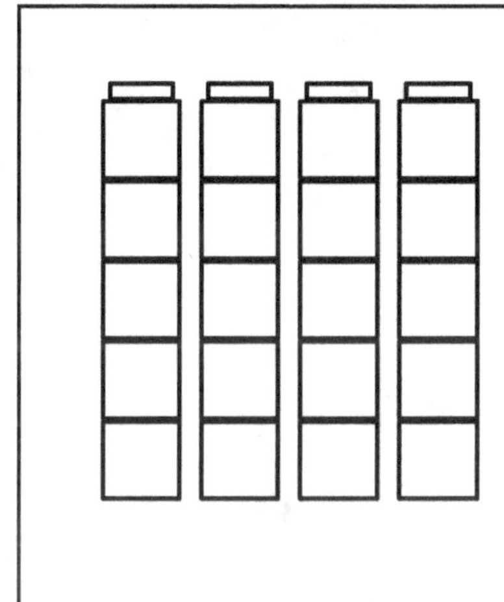

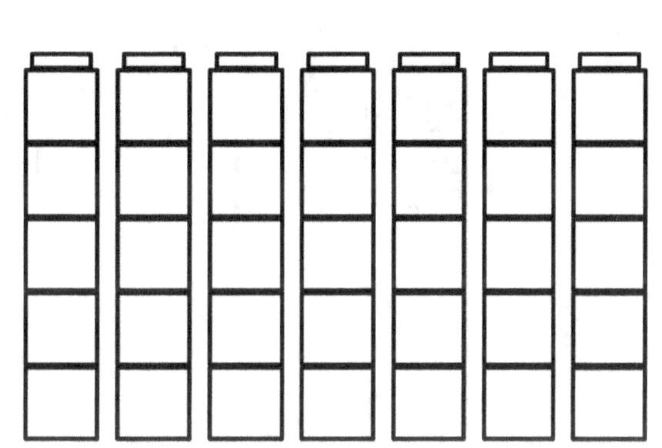

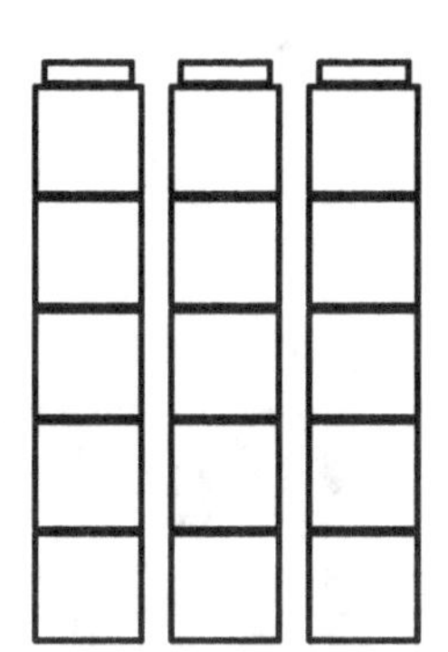

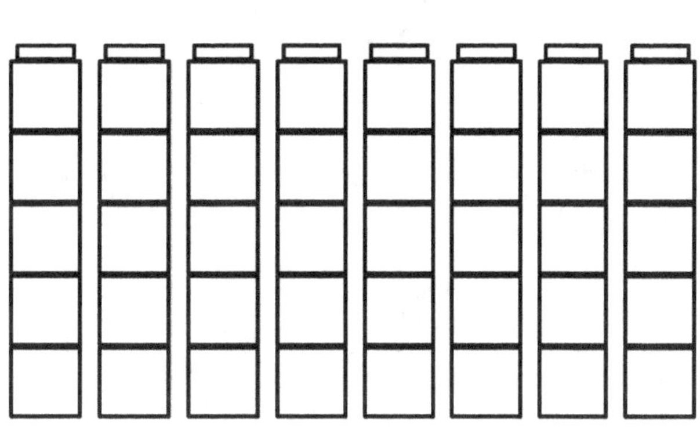

NAME _______________________   DATE _______________________

Morning or Evening?

Draw lines to connect the pictures to morning or evening.

Morning   **Evening**

More about 6

Trace the numbers. Fill in the missing numbers to complete the equations.

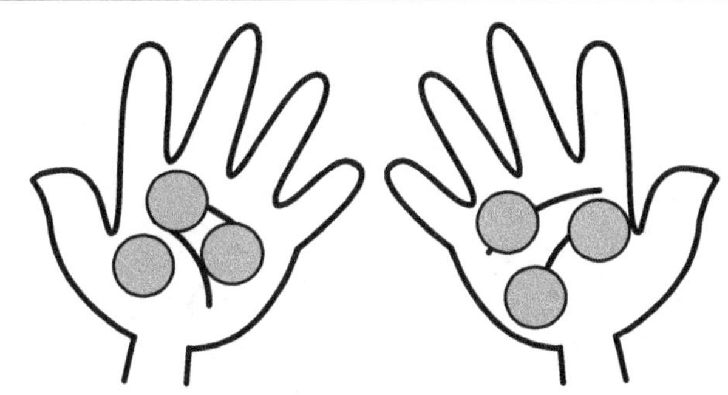

___ + ___ = 6

___ + ___ = 6

4 + ___ = 6

2 + ___ = 6

6 − 1 = 5

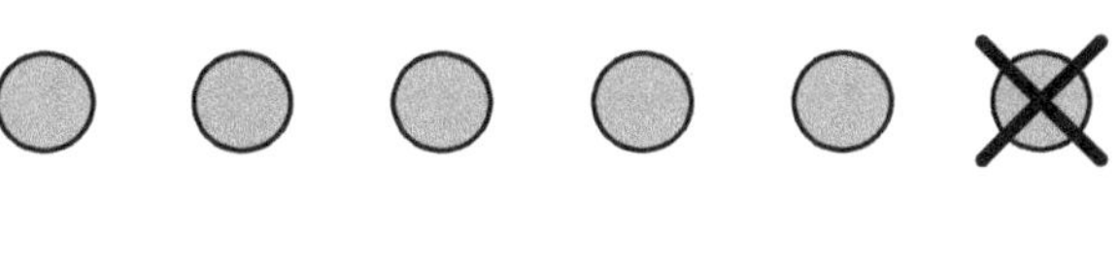

6 − 2 = 4

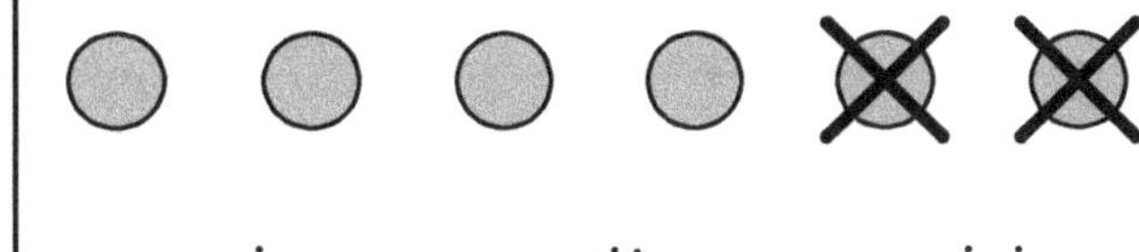

6 − 3 = 3

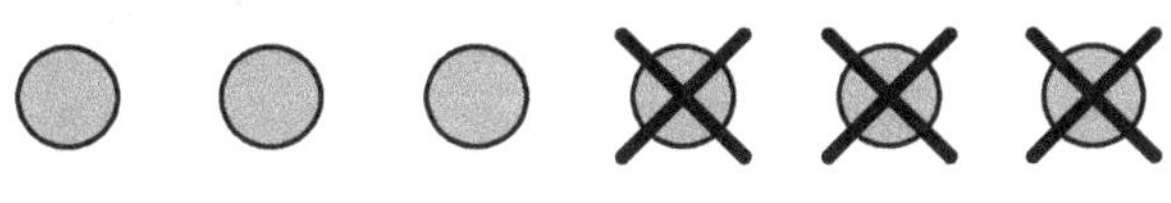

6 − 4 = 2

More or Less Time?

Circle the picture in each box that would take you *more* time.

The Frog Jumping Contest

1 Freddy Frog is practicing for the big frog jump contest. Color in the boxes to show how far he jumped each time.

1st Jump: 8 sticks

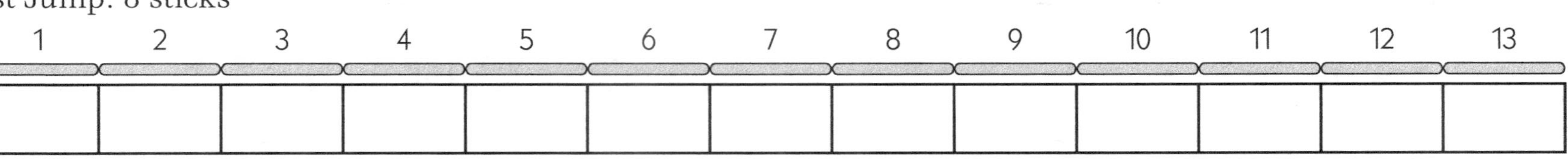

2nd Jump: 12 sticks

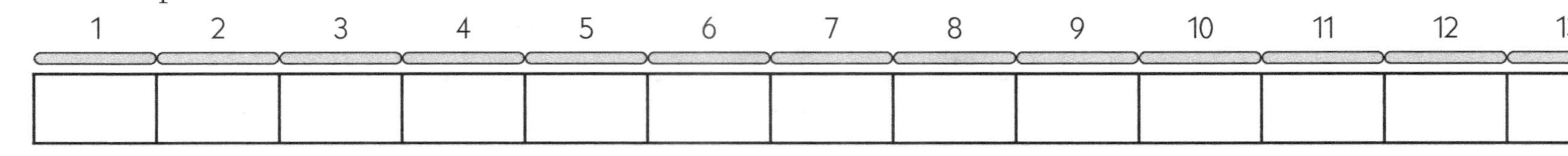

3rd Jump: 9 sticks

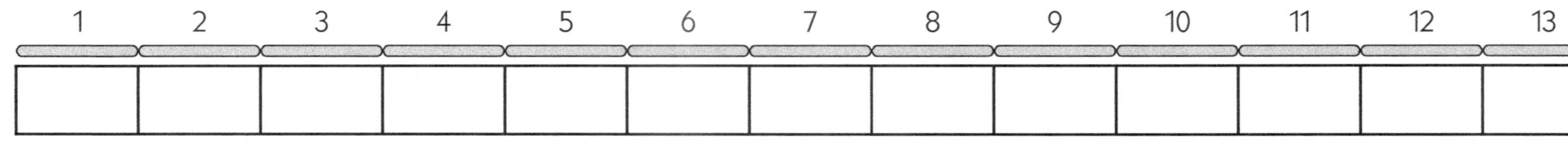

2 Which one was his longest jump? (Circle one.)   1st   2nd   3rd

3 Which one was his shortest jump? (Circle one.)   1st   2nd   3rd

Counting By Tens

1 Trace each number.

10   20   30   40   50   60   70   80

2 How many cubes?

Frog Addition

1 Color the frogs. Trace the numbers or symbols. Write an addition sentence to match the picture.

Color 2 frogs green. Color 3 frogs brown.

2 + 3 = _______

Color 4 frogs red. Color 1 frog blue.

_______ + _______ = _______

Color 3 frogs yellow. Color 2 frogs black.

_______ + _______ = _______

2 Add.

1	3	4	2	3	4
+ 2	+ 1	+ 1	+ 2	+ 2	+ 2

Frog Line-Up

1 The frogs are lined up for the big race! Color the frogs so it's easy to tell them apart.

- Color the 1st frog green.
- Color the 5th frog red.
- Color the 4th frog brown.
- Color the 3rd frog blue.
- Color the 2nd frog yellow.
- Color the 6th frog black.

2 Here is the race track. Fill in the missing numbers.

1		3		5		7		9	

3 Color in the boxes on the track.

- Color the 1st box red.
- Color the 7th box red.
- Color the 4th box red.
- Color the 6th box blue.
- Color the 3rd box blue.
- Color the 9th box blue.
- Color the 2nd box green.
- Color the 8th box green.
- Color the 5th box green.

4 What color should the 10th box be? _______________________ Color it in!

5 Add.

$$0 + 0 \qquad 0 + 1 \qquad 1 + 1 \qquad 2 + 1 \qquad 2 + 2 \qquad 2 + 3 \qquad 3 + 3$$

Frog Subtraction

1 Color the frogs. Trace the numbers or symbols. Write a subtraction sentence to match the picture.

Color 4 frogs green. Cross out 2 of them.

4 – 2 = ______

Color 5 frogs red. Cross out 1 of them.

5 – 1 = ______

Color 6 frogs brown. Cross out 3 of them.

______ – ______ = ______

2 Subtract.

2	3	4	5	5	6	6
− 1	− 2	− 2	− 3	− 4	− 1	− 2

Match the Shapes

Draw lines to match the shapes.

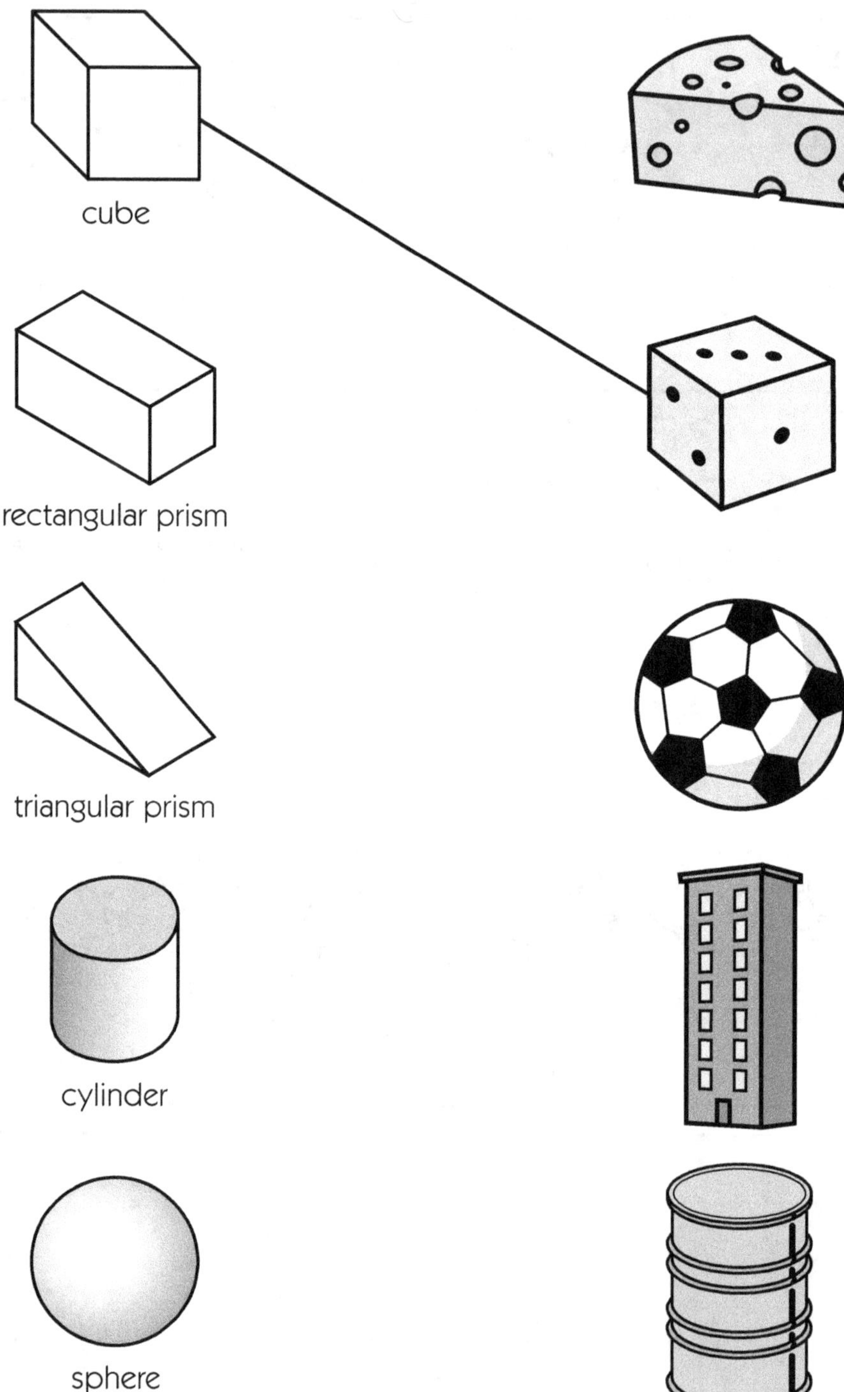